ST ANTONY'S PAPERS · NUMBER 13

★

THE RIGHT IN FRANCE

1890–1919

THREE STUDIES

ST ANTONY'S PAPERS

★

ST ANTONY'S PAPERS · NUMBER 13

THE RIGHT
IN FRANCE
1890–1919

Three Studies

EDITED BY

DAVID SHAPIRO

Southern Illinois University Press
Carbondale, Illinois

PUBLISHED BY
CHATTO AND WINDUS LTD
42 WILLIAM IV STREET
LONDON WC2

★

CLARKE, IRWIN AND CO LTD
TORONTO

★

LIBRARY OF CONGRESS CATALOG
CARD NUMBER 62–15227
FIRST AMERICAN EDITION

PRINTED IN GREAT BRITAIN BY
BUTLER AND TANNER LTD
FROME AND LONDON

CONTENTS

The main emphasis of the work of St Antony's College, Oxford, since its foundation in 1950 has been in the fields of modern history and international affairs. The College organizes a number of regular Seminars at which are read papers produced by its members in the course of their research or by visiting experts from other institutions. The College further sponsors the delivery of lectures in Oxford by scholars of international reputation in their respective fields.

An appreciable volume of contribution to scholarship is thus being produced under the auspices of St Antony's and the present series has been started in order to preserve and present a selection of this work. The series is not, however, confined to this material alone and includes contributions from other places.

Three numbers a year are issued and each number is devoted to a particular topic or a particular part of the world.

AUTHORS OF PAPERS

DAVID SHAPIRO read Greats at New College and the B.Phil. in European History at St Antony's College. He is now a Research Fellow of Nuffield College, Oxford.

D. R. WATSON read Modern History at Balliol College and the B.Phil. in European History at St Antony's College. He is now a Lecturer in Modern History in the Faculty of Social Science, Queen's College, Dundee, University of St Andrews.

MALCOLM ANDERSON read Modern History at University College and completed a D.Phil. in 1961. He is now an Assistant Lecturer in Government at the University of Manchester.

INTRODUCTION

AFTER 1877 the Right in France was excluded from effective political power. In the 1890's the rise of an organized socialist movement limited further the Right's freedom of manœuvre. Boulanger had been the last political figure to unite, although with difficulty, both Left and Right in protest against the Centre. The three studies in this volume are designed to illustrate the reaction of the Right to this new situation.

The dilemma that faced the adherents of the Right can be stated simply: if they indulged to the full their political preferences they could not but aid the subversion of the social and economic order that they wished to preserve; yet the preservation of that order seemed, at least in the period before the First World War, to entail supporting a political regime that they detested. In this situation they had to choose between parliamentary co-operation with the Centre and attempts to change the regime, whether violently by a coup, or legally by exploiting an issue that might win a popular majority. There were few on the Right who made a choice and consistently maintained it. For one thing conditions changed; more right-wing politicians would have been prepared to stake their future on anti-parliamentarism in 1899 than two years previously. Yet even the right-wing Nationalists at the height of their successes were still anxious to maintain their contacts with the Centre.

The behaviour of the politicians of the Right in this dilemma resembled that of the Left. On both sides principles were compromised to avert a greater evil. On both sides divisions opened between men inclined to compromise and those who were more fundamentalist. On the Left Millerand raised an issue by joining Waldeck-Rousseau's cabinet; on the Right the question was whether to vote for a government that included no politician of the Right. That this was, in one form or another, a constant problem for the Right should come as little surprise. There was a natural temptation to hedge the bet; revisionist candidates in 1889 could claim that they wished only to maintain the existing order, and the careful behaviour of Nationalist politicians in Paris after 1900 contrasts strongly with the antics of Déroulède. Furthermore circumstances could alter political dispositions and make intransigents of compromisers; Jacques Piou, the supple parliamentary strategist of the Ralliement in the early 1890's, was forced at times into rigid opposition by the anticlerical outburst that followed the Dreyfus Affair. The nature of the men on the Right and the

9

circumstances that they faced made them oscillate between compromise and intransigence. This oscillation paralleled that on the Left, and the play of both was the chief cause of the political instability of the Third Republic.

The studies in this volume attempt to explore the causes of the changes in right-wing attitudes and to show the effect on French politics of these changes. In doing so, they raise questions about two types of analyses of French politics, M. François Goguel's scheme of Third Republican politics and M. René Rémond's analysis of the Right.[1]

French political instability has always invited a structural analysis. M. Goguel has stressed the over-riding importance of the division between Left and Right. His critics have argued that the parliamentary politics of the Third Republic are intelligible only in terms of a Centre making temporary alliances, at one time with the Left, at another with the Right. To this he has replied that while the close relationships at the Centre may have been crucial for Chamber politics, these were never transferred to electoral politics; that indeed it is from this very fact that much of the political instability arose, and that the French electoral system of two ballots, at the second of which a simple plurality suffices, was bound to force electoral politics, and therefore the political feelings of the electorate, into two broad alignments. M. Goguel illustrates the endurance of these broad coalitions and the steadiness of their support by comparing the percentage of votes cast for supporters of MacMahon in 1877 – 45 per cent – and for *Poincaristes* in 1928 – $44\frac{1}{2}$ per cent.

There are two questions that the following studies raise about this analysis. Could the results of the intermediate elections, be interpreted to show such a high percentage for the Right? Between 1877 and 1928 a great section of what would have been considered in the Chamber of 1877 to be the Left passed over to the Right. Would, for example, the result of the elections of 1898 give M. Goguel such statistical satisfaction? Secondly, how far is it true that French electors refused to accept a tripartite division of political parties into Left, Centre and Right, and were forced by the electoral system to create two broad groupings of Left against Right. The relevant data have not been presented clearly. Most monographs that give detailed surveys of politics in the departments report election results in percentages gained by the Left and the

[1] F. Goguel, *La Politique des partis sous la IIIe République* (3rd edition, 1958).
R. Rémond, *La Droite en France de 1815 à nos jours; continuité et diversité d'une tradition politique* (1954).
All works published in Paris unless otherwise stated.

Right, terms not clearly defined. Doubt is cast on this mechanical application of M. Goguel's scheme wherever election results are reported in absolute figures, as for Côte d'Or; in that department the Right clearly practised the *politique du pire* in elections. M. Goguel's scheme of electoral politics cannot accommodate the notion of the *politique du pire*. This is emphasized by the failure of his theory, when applied in detail to the politics of the 1890's, to cast light on the electoral behaviour of the Right.

The answers to both questions raised above may bring back into favour the tripartite analysis of French politics to be found in the earlier works of André Siegfried. This provides a more satisfactory framework for M. Rémond's examination of tendencies within the Right, which sees the differences between Ultras, Orleanists and Bonapartists as replaced at the turn of the century by those between the supporters of the Ralliement, the Progressistes and the Nationalists. The material in this volume does not challenge M. Rémond's thesis, although it suggests some modifications in detail. If there is one general criticism it would be that M. Rémond over-emphasizes the break between 1873 and 1902. Is it true that between these dates the men, the names, the labels and the programmes changed? The analysis presented in the first study shows that there had been little change before 1898, at most only in the matter of labels; the men and the names had not changed but had been merely thinned out by electoral defeat, and the programmes made slightly more discreet. Many of the men on the Right in the 1890's were still playing the same role after 1905, not only leaders such as de Mun, Piou and Denys Cochin, but less notable deputies, a Jules Dansette, an Arthur Legrand. (The Index enables this continuity to be traced.) The social problems that engaged the real interests of the Right in 1906 differed not at all from those of 1894, and it is hard to see that the response changed.

We tend to assume that the structure of French politics was greatly altered in the years around 1900. It was Georges Sorel's pamphlet that first claimed the existence of *la Révolution Dreyfusienne*. Writing in 1909, towards the end of Clemenceau's ministry, Sorel argued that the consequences of the Affair had been the eclipse of one political class, the moderate Opportunists of the wealthy bourgeoisie; the "republican aristocracy" had been forced to appeal for support to the popular masses, and in so doing had had to yield power to politicians of a lower class. Yet the careers of Ribot, Poincaré and Barthou showed that this temporary trend was already being reversed by 1913. The political aftermath of the Dreyfus Affair seems now merely the last dying surge of a failing coalition, thankful to find an issue that masked essential differences on social and economic questions. The election to the Chamber of 50 Socialists in 1893 was a more significant indication of the change in the structure of French politics than the dramatic events of 1899. The Affair ended in the last great victory of Republican solidarity, and most participants played roles handed down from the early days of the Third Republic. But the Ralliement and the rise of socialism in the 1890's had already demonstrated that the future of French politics was on another course. The evolution of the Right, although some Orleanists had already in the 1870's rallied to the Republic, was largely a response to the new movements on the Left. This volume therefore passes over the efforts in the mid 1880's of Raoul Duval and Albert de Mun to change the character of right-wing politics, and considers the rise of new elements in the Right between 1890 and 1919.

DAVID SHAPIRO

THE RALLIEMENT IN THE POLITICS OF THE 1890's

by David Shapiro

I

". . . When the will of a people has been clearly declared, when the form of government has nothing in itself (as Leo XIII has recently declared) contrary to the sole principles by which Christian and civilized nations can live, since only a sincere adherence to the form of government can save the country from the horrors that threaten it, the time has come to . . . put an end to our divisions, to sacrifice all that conscience and honour allow . . ."

In these apparently innocuous terms the Archbishop of Algiers, Cardinal Lavigerie, addressed the company at a dinner given in honour of the French Mediterranean fleet. The response was icy; for the Cardinal was preaching acceptance of the Third Republic to a service notorious then as later for its lack of republican sentiment. The guest of honour, Vice-Admiral Duperré, an inveterate Bonapartist whose political convictions had only recently caused a stir, had to be prompted to reply: "I drink to his Eminence the Cardinal and to the clergy of Algeria." On official instructions the telegraphed agency report added to his reply a sentence of thanks for the Cardinal's speech. The Ralliement had begun inauspiciously.[1]

The Toast of Algiers of November 12, 1890, was made on the Vatican's initiative. In a survey of those whose attitudes, whether favourable or hostile, determined the outcome of the policy, it seems proper to begin by considering the motives of Leo XIII. Two of them were set forth in Lavigerie's speech, a desire that Catholics should accept the established form of government and should not at the end of the nineteenth century be opposing republican democracy as wrong in itself; secondly the wish to oppose socialism, "to save the world from the social peril", a need that inspired in politics the Ralliement, in social

[1] For the text of the Toast of Algiers, J. Tournier, *Le Cardinal Lavigerie et son action politique* (1913), pp. 287 ff.

13

and economic thought the encyclical *Rerum Novarum*. The third motive, which remained unacknowledged, was the Roman Question: Leo XIII still cherished the hope of undoing the work of September 20, 1870. The more immediate objectives of the Vatican were in French internal politics. For twenty years the defence of the Catholic church had been linked with the dying cause of monarchism; for fourteen years, at five successive general elections, the partisans of ideological resistance to any republic had failed to arouse popular enthusiasm for a church gradually stripped of much of its power. Nothing worse could follow from attempting a policy of conciliation.

Yet the Vatican was not a monolithic, utterly consistent maker of policy. There were many forces at work in Rome. The Sacred College was dominated by Italians, some of whom were not unreasonably concerned to reach agreement with Italy, a policy that ran counter in certain respects to that of the Ralliement. Sympathies were confused: for example, Cardinals Capecelatro and Parocchi, concerned with the promotion of biblical studies, were on this issue allies of some of the French Social Catholic supporters of the Ralliement; about the Ralliement the Cardinals as Italians were lukewarm, since they desired accommodation with Italy to draw the Italian clergy out of stagnation.[2] One group within the Vatican was simultaneously supporting d'Hulst on the issue of biblical studies against Decurtins, Didon, Boeglin and the Jesuits, and joining with the ralliés among the latter against the *refractaire* d'Hulst on the political issue.[3]

Equal disarray was to be found among the Catholic supporters of the Ralliement within France. They fell into three groups. First was a new, growing force, the Christian Democrats, turning eagerly to the working class, their most typical representatives being the abbés démocrates; they had inherited some of the Liberal Catholic tradition in politics, though not in economics. Then there were those politicians of the Right more concerned with social conservatism than with ideological monarchism. Thirdly, many devout Catholics both wished to obey the Pope and agreed that political conciliation would benefit the Church more than resistance to an established regime; this group included many adherents of the somewhat aristocratic Social Catholicism of La Tour du Pin and de Mun. This was an uneasy coalition. The conservative politicians were almost without exception liberals in their economic ideas; they looked askance, a laissez-faire economist like Leroy-

[2] J.-Ph. Heuzey-Goyau, *Georges Goyau* (1947), p. 111.
[3] *Ibid.*, pp. 116–17.

Beaulieu[4] even with trepidation, at the doctrines of *Rerum Novarum*. The Christian Democrats had considerable sympathy for those intransigent prelates who condemned the excesses of liberal economics; even Georges Goyau, the future academician, in 1892-3 a *normalien* studying in Rome and writing tracts on Social Catholicism, had a grudging admiration for Mgr. de Cabrières, Bishop of Montpellier, one of the most tenacious of the episcopal opponents of the Ralliement, who denounced laissez-faire doctrines.[5] The devout Catholics who supported the Ralliement in pious obedience to the Pope found it difficult to work with the other two forces. Liberal Catholics did not altogether relish the co-operation of *l'Univers* even under the editorship of Eugène Veuillot, the less virulent of the two brothers. The Catholic groups that promoted the Ralliement seemed to offer each a different road to salvation.

This did not make easier the task of co-operating with the right-wing Republicans, who alone were ready to enter into an accommodation with the Catholics. Ferry, Challemel-Lacour, Constans, Spuller, were men of principles akin to those of the conservatives weary of fruitless campaigns for a lost monarchist cause. Constans, speaking at Avignon in 1892 said: "Je suis un républicain de quarante ans de date. Depuis que j'ai soixante ans, je deviens un conservateur, mais conservateur républicain. (Laughter and applause.) Autrefois il n'y avait que les gens très bien qui fussent conservateurs. (Laughter and applause.) Notre tour est venu à nous aussi d'être des gens très bien. (Renewed laughter and applause.)" [6] Constans had shown in the liquidation of Boulangism that he could easily come to terms with a Mackau.[7] But with an abbé Lemire? For the latter, with the other two deputies termed "socialistes chrétiens", throughout the 1893-8 legislature tended to vote against the moderate conservatives on certain issues, and so could not be considered reliable supporters of, for example, the Méline cabinet.

The forces working against the success of the Ralliement were at first sight more formidable. French politics had come to be dominated by the struggle of a Republican coalition against the monarchist-clerical threat. On the Republican side this left a strong sentiment of

---

[4] *Ibid.*, pp. 111-12; cf. A. Leroy-Beaulieu, *La Papauté, le socialisme et la démocratie* (1892).

[5] J.-Ph. Heuzey-Goyau, *Georges Goyau*, p. 108.

[6] A. Dansette, *Histoire religieuse de la France contemporaine* (1952), ii, 176.

[7] A. Dansette, *Le Boulangisme* (1946), pp. 335-7.

concentration against the traditionalist Right, a sentiment only temporarily and only tacitly allayed in 1887 by the transient threat of external war. Among the Catholics there was bitter resentment of the *lois scolaires*, proclaimed even by the most conciliatory republicans to be untouchable – not surprisingly since Ferry, their author, was among the heralds of the new course in French politics. The Catholics could hope only that existing legislation would be applied more leniently, although its very existence contravened their most cherished principles; the conservative republicans mistrusted the sincerity of inveterate monarchists proclaiming their acceptance of the Republic – de Mun and Mackau had been deeply implicated in the Boulangist adventure – and feared for the safety of the republican *lois scolaires*, about which the ralliés openly proclaimed their reservations.

This atmosphere of suspicion was not the only obstacle to the Ralliement. As so often in French politics the extreme Right and the extreme Left wished to destroy the possibility of a strong Centre coalition.

The extreme Right was formed largely of intransigent monarchists. But another group should not be forgotten, those who may be termed by a not outrageous anachronism "integral" Catholics. The tag that the ralliés were those who were catholics before monarchists, the *refractaires* those who were monarchists before catholics, breaks down at this point. The internal history of the Catholic church has been dominated from the beginning of the nineteenth century by the dialogue between those who wished to accommodate, as far as faith allowed, with the modern world and those who wished to refuse any adaptation. Under the pontificate of Leo XIII, the papal influence was in the main for accommodation. Some of his opponents, sincere Catholics and Catholics before all else, were ready to coalesce temporarily with intransigent monarchists such as Emile Ollivier and Paul de Cassagnac.

The coalition of these two elements supplied the big battalions on the Right, some fifty odd deputies even after the electoral debacle of 1893, a tenth of the Chamber, thus grossly over-representing their real strength in the country; but in the Third Republic it was the individual deputy who mattered. That monarchism was dying they knew; only a handful dared to proclaim it in their electoral programmes. The rest were partisans of a more authoritarian state, some still sighed for the *juste milieu*. Emile Ollivier, the most respectable of their polemicists, was a republican converted to be a Premier of a Liberal Empire, who had become by ill-success a stubborn opponent of the Third Republic. Their opposition to the Ralliement was nourished by nationalist resentment of a Pope who canvassed support for Bismarck's Septennat and sought relief for Italian prisoners-of-war; it was encouraged by the successful and triumphant refusal of Leo XIII's political advice both by the Belgian Catholics and by the German Centre Party. But above all they were conservatives who wished for no compromise.

On the Left were the Radicals, the Radical-Socialists and the Socialists. The first two groups can be taken together; they represented as no other party the Frenchmen whose hearts were on the Left, but whose wallets . . . The joke does not do sufficient credit to the honour of their political beliefs. They were convinced, and not without cause, that political freedom would not be secure in France until the influence of the Catholic church had been extirpated. There was justice in their claim that the church had shown itself to be profoundly anti-democratic in France; in 1890 French democratic Catholics could recall the golden dawn of 1848 – and no more; incidents at elections in the West of France kept alive memories of past clerical pressure. But the Radicals were also uneasily aware that if the focus of politics shifted, they would have to take a definite stand on what was euphemistically termed "la question sociale". The dilemma was to be exposed during Clemenceau's government of 1906-9, it was put to them with eloquence in Jaurès' famous interpellation of Dupuy in November 1893. How much simpler for the Radicals would it be if the relations of church and state remained the centre of political controversy.

The Socialists might have followed the doctrine that the clerical issue was a bourgeois trap. Although Millerand sketched out such a line, that was intermittently followed by Jaurès, in time they came to adopt much the same attitudes as the Radicals. This for two reasons: anti-clericalism had taken too strong a hold on left-wing politics to be shaken off so quickly; secondly there is all the difference in the world between proclaiming the healthiness of a realignment of politics on social issues, between admitting, as a socialist, the need for a conservative party to encourage the formation of a socially left-wing party, and welcoming the success of a conservative government, such as Méline's, without trying to overthrow it. Yet the best means of defeating Méline seemed to be in the use of anticlericalism to revive the tradition of republican concentration.

The opposition to the new course in French politics came, at least initially, from the two extremes.

The Ralliement, opened with éclat by the Toast of Algiers, petered out with the fall of Méline's government. The hopes of a revival foundered in the Dreyfus affair with the suicide of Henry and the resignation of Cavaignac.

The first phase was from the Toast to the Papal encyclical of February 1892, *Au milieu des sollicitudes*, a time of uncertainty, more or less genuine, about papal intentions. Throughout the winter of 1890-1 the rival parties pleaded their cause at the Vatican, Freppel and Piou arriving within days of each other in February. By the end of 1891, in spite of the Gouthe-Soulard affair, played up by both the extreme Right and the Radicals, more and more Catholics were coming to accept the papal point of view. On February 17, 1892, *Le Petit Journal* published the interview of its editor, Judet, with Leo XIII; the first result was the overthrow of the Freycinet government by the two extremes in the Chamber.

From February 1892 until the general elections of August and September 1893 was a period of preparation and hope on the part of the ralliés. In the autumn of 1892 the dying Lavigerie could rejoice at the rallying of the episcopate to the new policy. The Union pour la France chrétienne had been dissolved in May, and de Mun had accepted Leo XIII's wishes ten days later. But although the monarchists[8] were in disorder, it remained more difficult to organize the ralliés for the 1893 elections. Goyau's letters[9] testify to Leo XIII's serious interest and to his impatience at the lack of progress. In general the monarchists maintained their candidatures in their fiefs, and left no pickings for the ralliés, many of whom were forced to appear as interlopers in their search for Catholic votes. The monarchists were reduced to some fifty, but on any definition the ralliés could muster barely thirty deputies.

The new Chamber reassembled with the ralliés' high hopes punctured. Yet it was in this period of political confusion, that lasted until the formation of the Méline government, that the successes of the two years 1896-8 were prepared. The electoral victory of the Socialists, who had gone out twelve and returned forty-eight, together with the mounting wave of anarchist outrages that culminated in the assassination of the President of the Republic, Sadi Carnot, in June 1894, demonstrated to all conservatives the need for unity. Spuller in a famous debate of March 1894 had called for "a new spirit" in the relations between Republicans and the Catholic Church, an end to mistrust and

---

[8] In contemporary usage 'monarchists' covered both Bonapartists and royalists; the latter term, both legitimists and orleanists.

[9] J.-Ph. Heuzey-Goyau, *Georges Goyau*, pp. 87 ff., 126-7.

18

petty harassing measures. Two issues remained, however, to be cleared away in the relations between church and state: the public inspection of the accounts of the vestries and the taxation levied on the religious orders. The first was settled without great fuss; the second was made the occasion of a display of intransigence—as a royalist journalist, asked by Cardinal Bourret what he hoped to gain by the outcry, explained: "Nothing: we are playing an air beneath the ministers' balcony to please the gallery." By the winter of 1895–6 the agitation had died down, and the attention even of the extreme Right was devoted to the platonic efforts of the Bourgeois government, France's first all-Radical cabinet, to push the Chamber into voting for an income tax.

The formation of the Méline ministry in April 1896 marked the fourth and triumphant phase of the Ralliement, the justification of the whole policy. It was the first cabinet since 1877 to rely on the votes of the Right almost without disguise. The *lois scolaires* were applied with a generous laxity, the laïcizing of public primary education was quietly forgotten. Clemenceau, meeting Piou in the lobbies of the Chamber in 1892, had remarked, "You should have adopted this policy twenty years ago; it is too late now, we have had too much of a head start. But if you have a hope, it is in the Vatican's policy." [10] For two years these hopes seemed justified. Then came the aftermath of the 1898 elections.

In retrospect it is easy to see that the course of the Dreyfus Affair would have doomed the Ralliement. But to judge of the policy's merits it is essential to examine the fall of the Méline ministry, which had nothing to do with the Affair: was it caused by popular revulsion against the new course in French politics, or was it the result of the mistakes of the coalition that supported Méline? How near to success was this attempt to substitute for a concentration of centres a sharp division of Right and Left as the dominant pattern of French politics?

A start to answering these questions must begin by examining politics in the Chamber of Deputies, where the Ralliement achieved its greatest success, and more particularly by examining the role of the Right in the Chamber of 1893–8: how far the deputies of the Right supported the Ralliement from the opening of the legislature, how far their attitude changed as the years, and governments, went by. The first task is to distinguish among the deputies of the Right the intransigents

[10] D. Ferrata, *Mémoires* (1920), ii, 51; a different version in J. Piou, *Le Ralliement* (1928), pp. 27–8.

and the ralliés. A comparison of the social, economic and political background of the two groups gives some idea of the fine balance of conflicting allegiances on the Right in the 1890's. This impression is confirmed by a study of the Right's voting record in the 1893-8 Chamber. Finally a survey of the Ralliement in the constituencies throws light on the greatest failure of those who hoped to set French politics on a new course

II

Deputies had formed groups from the beginning of the Third Republic, but not until 1910 was notice officially taken of the group's existence. Before that date it has been found difficult to classify deputies.[11] The Right in the 1893-8 Chamber presents additional hazards: the groups formed in 1893 did not maintain themselves, and many members came to change their tactics within three years. In order to study this movement of opinion, some method must be found to determine the deputies' intentions at the time of their election.

One instrument lies to hand. In 1881 an ardent Republican deputy, Barodet, persuaded the Chamber to order the collection "of the authentic texts of the electoral programmes and engagements" of the deputies returned at the general election of that year. The same proposal was adopted in 1885, and the habit thus acquired has lasted to the present day. Barodet's purpose had been to give the public some yardstick by which to judge the conduct of deputies during the course of the legislature, and to force the deputies either not to make rash claims or to try to justify them. The thick quarto volumes that perpetuate his name have served at least to demonstrate the conventions governing the choice of slogans in French electoral propaganda. The general principle, that these election addresses "while lacking the sincerity of an intimate confession make perfectly clear the nuance the candidate wished to express", was stated by André Siegfried.[12] By the choice of his slogans in 1893 or 1898 a rallié distiuguished himself from an intransigent.

---

[11] A. Bomier-Landowski, "Les groupes parlementaires . . .", in F. Goguel, G. Dupeux, *Sociologie électorale* (1951), pp. 75–89, who appears not to have used the contemporary article by A. Salles cited below. F. Goguel, *Géographie des élections françaises* (1951), p. 28, notes the particular difficulty in identifying the ralliés in the 1893 elections.

[12] A. Siegfried, *Tableau politique de la France de l'Ouest sous la Troisième République* (1913), pp. xvii–xviii.

But before these two groups can be separated, the whole of the Right must be marked off from its neighbours in the Centre. In 1893 this was still a relatively sharp division. The general elections of 1889 had been fought by the Right on the question of the regime, against the Republic. Any candidate in that election had to declare himself on the issue, and nearly all those who sat in the 1893-8 legislature had been candidates in 1889. There remain one or two deputies, some of whom had entered politics in the 1890's, who are assigned by some contemporary authorities, l'Année Politique (1893), l'Annuaire de la Presse française (1895) and A. S. Grenier, Nos députés, 1893-1898, to the group of ralliés; these three sources would add a further sixteen deputies to the list of twenty-five compiled by A. Salles for the April 1898 issue of the Revue politique et parlementaire.

The twenty-five listed by A. Salles are indubitably of the Right; the policy of the journal for which he compiled an analysis of deputies and their voting records was to encourage the conservative republicans and to play down the importance of the ralliés. Among the sixteen suggested additions, seven should be accepted: Vogüé—in listing as a republican a rallié star,[13] Salles reveals his preoccupations—d'Alsace, who had stood as a revisionist in 1889, Fould, who in 1889 signed his election address "candidat revisionniste conservateur", Sébastien Gavini, as a member of a notoriously Bonapartist family with a close relative an undoubted rallié, Loyer, a cotton-spinner from Lille who felt it necessary both in 1893 and 1898 to stress the sincerity of his loyalty to the Republic, de Saint-Quentin, who entered the Chamber at a by-election in 1896, on the word of André Siegfried,[14] and Wignacourt as a monarchist candidate of 1889. The remaining nine, Alicot, Jules Brice, Luce de Casabianca, Ducos, Dumas, Paul Lebaudy, Marcel-Habert, Morillot and Sonnery-Martin, either have some justification for claiming that they were republicans, at least by 1889, or, belonging to the remnants of Boulangism, have fallen victim to a whim of the writer of l'Année Politique.

If the line of division is drawn as above, one hundred and one of the deputies who sat in the 1893-8 legislature are to be classified as belonging to the Right. Of the hundred and one, ten died, one resigned and one was elected to the Senate in the course of the legislature, while fifteen, of whom one died in January 1898, entered at by-elections. Thus

[13] J.-Ph. Heuzey-Goyau, Georges Goyau, pp. 87, 126-8, for Leo XIII's hopes of Vogüé.
[14] Op. cit., p. 323.

the Right returned eighty-six strong in 1893, but were eighty-nine when the Chamber dissolved.

The material in the "Barodets" for the elections of 1889, 1893 and 1898 suffices to separate the ralliés from the intransigents. The volume for 1893 omits the programmes of only fourteen of the hundred and one deputies of the Right. The opinions of the two who died before the publication of the "Barodet", Abrial and Kermenguy, can be inferred from their past. Of the twelve elected at by-elections after the publication,[15] six, Baron, L'Estourbeillon, Du Halgouet, Savary de Beauregard, Dansette and Saint-Quentin were re-elected in 1898; for them we have at least their 1898 programmes. Derrien cited in 1898 his previous programme at some length. Gayraud's is to be found in the report of the commission appointed to enquire into the circumstances of his election.[16] La Biliais had had a long political career. For only three, colonel d'Aillières, Beauregard and Raoul Des Rotours is comparable material lacking.

This trivial lack of completeness is not the major difficulty. In the 1890's deputies of the extreme Right became more and more hesitant about expressing their convictions. Of the eighty-six deputies of the Right elected in 1893, thirty-three had made some reference to their monarchist convictions;[17] in 1898 only nine did so, a drop even when allowance is made for the death of seven, and the defeat or retirement of eight of those who had proclaimed their monarchist faith in 1893. The remainder of the monarchists must be sought under other guises, to be distinguished from the ralliés by the tone of their remarks about the Republic.

The key phrases of a rallié election address were employed most succinctly in 1893 by prince d'Arenberg:

> Dés 1889, je m'étais franchement placé sur le terrain constitutionnel . . . Quel est le Français, quel est le conservateur qui ne serait heureux de . . . fonder une République honnête, ouverte at tolérante?

Add to that a sentence from his address of 1898:

> Cette adhésion, je l'ai donnée sans arrière-pensée et j'ai loyalement et fidèlement servi le gouvernement de la République.

[15] The programmes of d'Alsace, de Mun and baron André Reille are included.

[16] *Impressions parlementaires. Chambre. 6e législature*, Vol. 47, No. 2451 (annexe au procès-verbal de la séance du 24 mai 1897).

[17] Du Bodan, Kergariou, La Ferronnays, Lorois and Rohan issued no electoral statement whatsoever; their views were well known.

The two phrases "terrain constitutionnel" and "adhésion . . . sans arrière-pensée" are the sure signs of a rallié. The most uncompromising intransigent could well demand "une République honnête" just after the revelations of the Panama scandal, but the addition of "ouverte" or "tolérante" took some of the sting out of the demand. In 1893 six of the elected right-wing deputies referred explicitly to the Pope, five of them making clear their support of the Ralliement.[18] Finally, a reference to a "droite indépendante" or a "droite républicaine" also denotes a rallié.

These criteria yield a compact group of twenty-seven of those elected in 1893.[19] To them must be added those ralliés who showed their adherence to the Republic by using republican rather than rallié terminology, Sebastien Gavini and Loyer, and seven of those who won by-elections, d'Alsace, Dansette, Gayraud, de Mun, baron André Reille, Raoul Des Rotours as the son of his father, and Saint-Quentin. Lastly, Charles Balsan, who used the full flower of rallié slogans in 1898, contented himself in 1893 with saying:

> C'est ainsi que, ennemi de toute opposition de parti pris, approuvant le bien sans demander quel en est l'auteur, j'ai donné mon concours au Gouvernement, quand il a proposé des mesures que je jugeais conformes aux intérêts de la nation.

He might be allowed to bring the total up to thirty-seven. Of them thirty were elected in 1893, seven at by-elections, and two died before the 1898 elections.

Hard against these must be set the thirty-three who proclaimed in 1893 their monarchist convictions.[20] In addition, Cibiel in 1898

---

[18] The sixth, Mgr. d'Hulst, Rector of the Institut catholique of Paris, displayed an attitude of mind worth noting:

"La forme du gouvernement n'est plus contestée. Parmi les catholiques, les uns, cédant à d'augustes conseils, acceptent la République comme le régime définitif de la France moderne; les autres, persuadés qu'elle marque, non le terme final, mais une phase temporaire de l'évolution démocratique, réservent leurs préférences pour l'avenir, mais ne veulent attendre que de la libre volonté de la nation le changement qu'ils espèrent. Les uns et les autres sont donc respectueux de la Constitution."

[19] Adam, d'Arenberg, Berry, Brincard, Desjardins, Dupuytrem, Dussaussoy, Elva, Fould, Antoine Gavini, Grandmaison, Jaluzot, Le Gavrian, Lemire, Montalembert, Montfort, Passy, Paulmier, Plichon, baron René Reille, Robert-Eugène Des Rotours, Schneider, Amaury Simon, Tailliandier, Viellard, Vogüé, Wignacourt.

[20] Arnous, Baudry d'Asson, Bernis, Paul Bourgeois, Broglie, Cazenove de Pradine, Colbert-Laplace, Du Bodan, Gamard, Gautier, Gellibert des Seguins,

referred to the "préférences personelles" which he had not abandoned while supporting a government which kept out the Radical-Socialists; Denys Cochin and baron Gérard in 1898 also announced that they had not abandoned their political convictions; two of those who had entered the Chamber at by-elections, Baron and Derrien, at the 1898 general elections, both claimed they had not abandoned their personal convictions in supporting the Méline cabinet. The total of avowed monarchists is thirty-eight. Their avowals vary in discretion from Baudry d'Asson, who ended his address:

> Fidélité! Fidélité! Fidélité! Ce que pour moi voulait dire: Dieu! France! Monarchie!

to Ornano, whose fiery Bonapartism was hardly conspicuous in the declaration that

> La République existe . . . je travaille à la purifier, à la gouverner. La Constitution de 1875 est revisable . . .

The remaining twenty-six deputies of the Right, who fall between the two groups of explicit ralliés and avowed monarchists, must be examined in more detail. A number of them proclaimed in 1893 that the Republic was no longer in question, but added such devastating criticisms of past Republican governments that no elector would have supposed that they would give consistent support to a conservative, if Republican, cabinet. Henry Cochin, Delafosse, Dufaure, Galpin declaring "Si je ne veux pas être un factieux, je ne suis pas un courtisan", Hugues whose claim "Je suis un indépendant et non un 'résigné'" may be accepted, La Noue, Levis-Mirepoix, Mackau, Pontbriand ("Pour Dieu et pour la France!"), Serph, all qualified acceptance of the Republic with demands that they knew no republican would meet. Some confined their remarks on the issue of the constitution to a claim that the idea of systematic opposition was far from their minds, a claim that on the Right in the 1890's was not made except by deputies on whom suspicion could plausibly fasten; Augustin d'Aillières, Fouquet, Porteu ("aussi éloigné de l'opposition systématique que résolu à protester contre les entreprises déshonnêtes"), Rauline ("Je ne suis pas, vous le savez, un homme d'opposition systématique") and Villiers, made use

Gonidec de Traissan, Mgr. d'Hulst, Juigné, Kergariou, La Bourdonnaye, La Ferronnays, Lanjuinais, Largentaye, La Rochejaquelein, Laroche-Joubert, Le Cerf, Arthur Legrand, Lorois, Maillé, Maurice-Binder, Ornano, Prax-Paris, Ramel, Rohan, Saint-Martin-Valogne, Soland, Witt.

of this pleasing political convention that was designed to deceive those who wished to be. A few, thinking it indiscreet to mention convictions that, while acceptable in their constituencies, were finding less and less favour in France as a whole, preferred to pass over in silence the question of the regime. But the constituents of Bougère, deputy for the arrondissement of Segré (Maine-et-Loire),[21] of La Rochefoucauld who claimed confidently "Vous me connaissez tous", and of Trevéneuc, could have had few doubts about the real political leanings of their deputies. Two deputies, Abrial and Kermenguy died within months of their election, and their electoral statements are not recorded. It is difficult to imagine that Kermenguy, a *chevau-léger* of the National Assembly, would have accepted the Ralliement. Abrial, a monarchist deputy from 1884 to 1885, who in 1889 as a revisionist had defeated Jaurès, cannot be assigned so surely; in the absence of any evidence to the contrary he should be reckoned as intransigent.

Finally six of those who entered the Chamber at by-elections can also be considered intransigents, although with less certainty than Baron and Derrien, mentioned above, who proclaimed themselves monarchists in 1898. Colonel d'Aillières succeeded his nephew in 1897 and disappeared from political life together with his constituency in 1898; in the absence of evidence he is to be classed with his nephew. Beauregard, elected in 1897 and defeated a year later, leaves no trace in the "Barodets"; A. Salles put him with the intransigent Right. La Biliais was a legitimist deputy from 1876 until 1889, when he gave up his constituency to Cazenove de Pradine; on the latter's death in 1896 he was re-elected, to be defeated in 1898, not having changed the opinions of his youth and middle age. L'Estourbeillon, Du Halgouet and Savary de Beauregard, re-elected in 1898, can be judged on their 1898 election programmes, which have nothing good to say for the Méline cabinet. Savary de Beauregard declared:

> Je ne me suis jamais preoccupé de savoir si telle proposition était soutenue par un ami ou par un adversaire, par le Gouvernement ou par l'opposition.

He had always voted according to his conscience during his seven months as a deputy. But the policy of the Ralliement demanded that he should be concerned to support a government such as Méline's. Savary de Beauregard brings the total of intransigents to sixty-four. Of them fifty-six were elected in 1893 and eight at by-elections; during the

[21] A. Siegfried, *Tableau politique de la France de l'Ouest*, pp. 68–9.

legislature eight died, one resigned and one was elected to the Senate.

Thus the hundred and one deputies of the Right fall into two groups, thirty-seven ralliés and sixty-four intransigents.

The election addresses preserved in the "Barodets" serve not only to distinguish rallié from intransigent; they also reflect some aspects of French politics in the 1890's. The first impression is one of continuity. The slogans of a rallié in 1893 are often versions, very slightly watered down, of what had been proclaimed by a faint-hearted revisionist in 1889. More than half the intransigents elected in 1893 made no secret of their monarchism; the four previous years had made their statements perhaps a trifle more wistful. Secondly there was a hard core of intransigence that did not bode well for the success of the Ralliement. More menacing than the bluster of a Baudry d'Asson was the intellectual certainty of Mgr. d'Hulst, prelate of the Church, openly if not blatantly disagreeing with the Sovereign Pontiff. Yet some comfort could be found in the absence of a sharp dividing line between the two groups. Little separated an avowed monarchist from an intransigent who chose not to raise explicitly the question of the regime, and little separated the latter from a rallié. An extremist might come by small stages to support the Ralliement; if things were to go wrong the reverse could easily happen. The Toast of Algiers had been a call to decisive action; the policy if successful would change dramatically the course of French politics. The response of the Right was slow, by no means entirely favourable. Thirty of the deputies elected in 1893 were committed to the Ralliement; they could expect others of the Right to help them, judging by the tone of election addresses. But for all the deputies of the Right the choice between intransigence and the Ralliement seems to have been very finely balanced. This impression is confirmed if we turn to study the personal background of the deputies who made, or refused to face, this choice.

III

The private diaries and memoirs that might explain the motives of these deputies have not been published. In their absence only certain questions can be answered. The two groups, ralliés and intransigents, can be compared only for a limited range of characteristics: age, together with the length of their parliamentary service; their advanced education, if any, and their occupations; their local and family connections; and their political antecedents.

Material for these comparisons comes from three types of sources, manuscripts in the archives of the Chamber of Deputies, collective biographies of deputies, and certain works by left-wing writers on the business interests of deputies.

The manuscript material is disappointing. For each legislature there exists the *Relevés de l'état civil des Députés*, those for the sixth legislature (1893–8) being bound in two volumes. To each deputy was sent a sheet of paper headed "Chambre des Députés. Archives" with his name and department already inserted. The deputy was asked to fill in his "Prénoms, Date de naissance, Lieu de naissance, Qualités" and then to sign the sheet. The business was not taken very seriously; twenty-four of the deputies of the Right failed to fill up their sheet, and those that did often left a blank after "Qualités". Brincard scribbled "nombreuses" in pencil after "Qualités", Desjardins scrawled "meme chose" in red crayon across the whole sheet and was noted as "Refusé". On each sheet is pasted in the top right-hand corner a photograph, and in the bottom left-hand corner a printed account of the deputy's career. The printed notice always, and the photograph except in the few cases where the deputy supplied his own, are taken from a work by A. S. Grenier, *Nos députés 1893–1898*, published at Paris, undated but on internal evidence during 1894; for this reason nothing is pasted on the sheets of deputies elected after the beginning of 1894.

Most of the information is therefore drawn from printed works of biography. The hundred years up to 1889 is covered by Robert and Cougny, *Dictionnaire des parlementaires français*; the deputies of the period 1900–14 are recorded in Samuel and Bonet-Maury, *Les Parlementaires français*, Vol. II. The 1893–8 legislature falls within the gap, which is filled by A. S. Grenier, who published volumes entitled *Nos députés* shortly after the elections of 1893 and 1898, and by Alphonse Bertrand, who produced three similar works after the elections of 1889, 1893 and 1898. Grenier's series are small volumes that have for each deputy a photograph and two or three lines listing qualifications, posts, etc. Bertrand wrote at greater length, averaging an octavo page for each deputy. Additional information, especially on deputies of the Right, is to be found in the works published after the elections of 1871, 1877, 1885 and 1889 by Félix Ribeyre, a convinced monarchist who takes little trouble to disguise his sympathies.

In general these sources mention the business interests of the deputies, but some further details can be gleaned from the works of Auguste Chirac, R. Mennevée and Augustin Hamon. Chirac[22] listed for the early 1880's the interests of fifty-two senators and ninety-three deputies, some of whom are to be found still sitting on the Right in the 1890's. Augustin Hamon began writing in Chirac's genre in the late 1880's, turned aside to translate Shaw into French, but in his old age produced three volumes, *Les Maîtres de la France*, that contain some material on the deputies of the 1890's. All these works are tendentious, and suffer from the fact that their authors were not on visiting terms with the families whose intricate relationships they sought to unravel.

Since the Ralliement was an attempt to alter the traditional structure of French politics, it might be expected that it should have appealed more to a younger generation, and that this should have been reflected in the ages of the rallié deputies. The average age on December 31, 1893, of the thirty elected in August of that year was rather under forty-six. Of the fifty-six intransigents elected the average age was just over fifty-three and a half. Of the fourteen deputies of the Right under forty, nine were ralliés, of the twenty aged sixty or over only three were ralliés.

More striking than the disparity of ages is the difference between political generations. The thirty ralliés returned at the general elections of 1893 had had an average parliamentary experience of slightly over five years, the fifty-six intransigents of just under twelve and a half years. While thirty-one of the intransigents – more than half – had first been elected to the Chamber before 1885, only four of the ralliés had had an equally long career as a deputy. Only eight of the ralliés had been deputies before 1889, the year of the final monarchist debacle. The distinguishing feature of the intransigents was their maintenance of a tradition of French politics of the 1870's and 1880's that attracted few but its past adherents. They did not maintain their numbers during the legislature, and two of their eight successful by-election candidates were over sixty at the time of their election.

Only in considering the age structure of the two groups does it seem necessary to distinguish between those elected in August 1893 and the winners of by-elections. Henceforward, except in studying their regional distribution, calculations are based on the two groups of sixty-four intransigents and thirty-seven ralliés, a proportion of roughly two to one.

[22] *L'Agiotage sous la IIIe République*, 1888, Vol. II, pp. 4–9.

Details of education are not easy to come by; the secondary school of only two deputies, Trevéneuc and Lemire, is recorded in sources consulted. Altogether at least fifty-eight of the hundred and one, thirty-seven intransigents and twenty-one ralliés had received some form of university education; the proportions within each group are broadly similar. The majority of these, thirty-six – ten of them ralliés – had degrees in law; twelve, seven of them ralliés, had passed out of St. Cyr. Except for St. Cyr the "grandes écoles" were represented only by two *polytechniciens*, Fouquet and Du Halgouët, both intransigents, and by two graduates of the Ecole Centrale, Le Gavrian and Plichon, both ralliés.

Significant patterns begin to emerge when we turn to the deputies' occupations. Almost all must have been *propriétaires*; all but thirty-four are so described, and where this description is omitted, as in the case of baron René Reille who had vast estates in his constituency, it is often because the fact was well known or added little to the impression of his standing. The army, excluding the many who saw service in the winter of 1870-1, was represented by eight ralliés and seven intransigents, a disproportion of no obvious import. But a difference emerges in the numbers of former diplomats and civil servants: the ralliés included only one of the six former diplomats, and one out of the eleven who had held administrative posts in the civil service or Conseil d'Etat. The Republican purge of the administration, which began in 1879, was early enough not to affect many of a group whose average age in 1879, was nearly forty-six. It is natural to find that those whose careers had been ended in this purge should have been among the intransigents.

Twenty-four right-wing deputies were industrialists, company directors or bankers, nine of them intransigents. The other fifteen supplied nearly half of the ralliés' strength. This makes political sense. They were men whose fortunes were most closely linked to the preservation of public order. Political crisis was bad for business, less so for landowners. The Schneiders, owners of the great engineering works of Le Creusot, had little stomach for political adventure: Paul-Henri, elected in 1889 as a revisionist "mais déclarant qu'il ne visait qu'à assurer l'ordre", was clearly happy to write in his 1893 election address that the past four years had further strengthened his desire for order and his aversion from political intrigues. On his retirement in 1898 his son, Charles, presented himself to represent the family and the constituency of Autun II; naturally roused by the Dreyfus case, he demanded that the army and navy should be protected by the respect of all against the injustices of party spirit, slipping in a phrase, not found in most right-wing addresses, on the need for powerful armaments. Why should one of the great manufacturers of armaments be an intransigent?

Nine of the intransigents did have some connection with the world of business. Bougère, described as a banker and industrialist was an administrator of the Caisse de l'Epargne et de Prévoyance de la ville d'Angers (*Relevés*). Cibiel, described as an industrialist with mining interests, is stated by Chirac to have had a major holding in Houillières et fonderies de l'Aveyron. Fouquet managed a brass-wire factory at Rugles (Eure). Gautier, who described himself in the *Relevés* as a "rentier", is noted by Chirac as being concerned in the direction of the Chemin de Fer d'Orléans. Baron Gérard was a director of the Chemins de Fer de l'Ouest, and, according to Chirac, of the Eaux and Houillières de la H^{te} Loire. Laroche-Joubert inherited from his father, as well as his constituency, a large paper manufacturing concern at Angoulême; he was also an administrator of the Bank of France. Maillé was an iron-master, whose time was probably more taken up by being a *propriétaire* in Maine-et-Loire, where he presided over the *conseil général* and which elected him to the Senate in 1896. Porteu owned a cotton mill at Rennes. Witt is said by Hamon to have been made in 1883 a director of the Anzin mining company. Of these nine only Laroche-Joubert, and possibly Maillé, was a major industrialist; baron Gérard and Witt were ornamental figures, Witt bound up with the improvement of his estates in Normandy.

Among the ralliés were men of more substance and power in the French economy. Adam was the third-generation head of a family bank that had prospered in the industrialization of the North of France. Prince d'Arenberg was a director of Anzin and became in 1896 president of the administrative council of the Suez Company. Balsan, who managed at Châteauroux "la fabrique de draps de troupe . . . la plus ancienne et la plus considérable qu'il y ait en France", was a Regent of the Bank of France from 1891 to 1913. Brincard owned in his constituency a sugar factory as well as large agricultural and forest estates. Fould, the grandson of Napoleon III's minister, had banking interests. Jules Jaluzot was a founder and a principal shareholder of the Grands-magasins du Printemps, a landowner in Nièvre where he owned various factories, and "boasted of giving work to more than 10,000 people". Le Gavrian had inherited when still in his twenties a machinery firm at Lille, from the active management of which he had retired in 1882. Loyer, also from Lille, was a cotton spinner. Passy was a director

of Crédit Foncier de France, Crédit Foncier colonial, Crédit industriel
et commercial, and of the Banque Centrale du travail et de l'épargne.
Plichon had interests in the Mines de Béthune. Baron René Reille was
the most notable industrial magnate among the deputies of the Right:
president of the administrative council of the Mines de Carmaux, president of the Comité des forges at some time during the 1890's, he was
also on the boards, according to Chirac, of the Chemins de Fer de l'Est,
Eaux de la banlieue de Paris and Forges et fonderies d'Alais. Baron
Robert-Eugène Des Rotours owned important sugar factories in Nord.
Paul-Henri Schneider not only owned the Usines Métallurgiques du
Creusot, but was also a Regent of the Bank of France and a director of
the Chemin de Fer d'Orléans. Amaury Simon is described as a major
industrialist. Viellard was an ironmaster from Belfort, who became a
director of the Suez Company. These were men who had prospered under the Republic and stood to lose heavily in a period of
political uncertainty that would follow an attempt to change the regime,
whether successful or not.

The connection between industry and the rallié deputies is marked
also in the regional distribution of the seats held by the Right after the
elections of 1893. The two departments of Nord and Pas-de-Calais, the
only major industrial area that could be termed Catholic, returned nine
of the thirty ralliés and one, Henry Cochin, of the fifty-six intransigents.
In the West of France, as defined by Siegfried, thirty-nine intransigents
were elected to six ralliés, three of whom came from traditionally
Orleanist Normandy. The fifteen remaining ralliés were scattered over
the whole country; Viellard was the solitary representative of the
Right in the East, a Republican stronghold not yet shaken by the
Dreyfus Affair. The sixteen intransigents who did not come from the
West or the department of Nord, sat for the two wealthiest areas of Paris,
the region of intense Catholicism on the southern edge of the Massif
central, and Charente where five Bonapartists were still entrenched.

Turning now to the more local connections of these deputies, and
examining all the hundred and one who sat at any time during the
1893–8 legislature, it is at once apparent that carpet-bagging found
little favour. Only three deputies, de Mun in Morlaix II and Mgr.
d'Hulst and Gayraud in Brest III, neighbouring constituencies in
Finistère, had no personal or family ties with the department. They
had been chosen as deputies for the most clerical area in France by the
last remaining grand electors, the priests of Léon.

For the rest, at least seventy-three, forty-eight intransigents and twenty-five ralliés, were *conseillers généraux* of their department. Forty-nine, thirty intransigents and nineteen ralliés, had been born in the department they represented; the other thirty-four intransigents and eighteen ralliés were divided equally between those born in Paris, and those born elsewhere. Those not recorded as holding some local elective office total fourteen: seven ralliés, Gayraud and de Mun mentioned above, Lemire who was a priest with an academic post in his constituency, Desjardins, Jaluzot – "giving work to 10,000" serves the same purpose – Le Gavrian, a vice-president of the Lille Chamber of Commerce, and Vogüé, of all the ralliés the most amateur politician; the seven intransigents were Mgr. d'Hulst, mentioned above, colonel d'Aillières, on whom informations is lacking, Delafosse, the founder-owner of the newspaper *Ami de l'Ordre* at Caen, Dufaure, Gamard, a *conseiller municipal* of Paris for twelve years before winning the seat in which stood his country property, Hugues, and Trevéneuc. Both intransigents and ralliés were local notables.

Neither group could claim that they were "hommes nouveaux". Seventeen ralliés could trace a relationship to one or more past deputies of their department; three had inherited their constituency directly. Among the intransigents the corresponding figures were sixteen and four; to them must be added four whose ancestors had sat for other departments. While a rallié deputy was more likely to have a deputy among his ancestors, it was the intransigents who had the pedigrees.

This suggests that the intransigents were the remnants of the legitimists. It seems plausible to consider the policy of the Ralliement, on the other hand, as typically Orleanist. The tripartite division into legitimists, Orleanists and Bonapartists became less watertight as the Republic established itself. Nevertheless for all but seven of the intransigents, and for half of the ralliés, a guess can be made, based on some information either about the deputy's role in the 1870's or about a relative's career under the Second Empire. Like father, like son, may not always be true; not all official candidates under the Second Empire were Bonapartists; the figures may err in detail.

Most strikingly they bear out the impression given by the preponderance of nobility among the intransigents. Twenty-six can plausibly be termed legitimist, among the ralliés only d'Arenberg and de Mun.[23]

[23] René Rémond, *La Droite en France de 1815 à nos jours* (1954), p. 157, states: "La droite ralliée est composée d'anciens monarchistes, plus souvent de tradition légitimiste que de filiation orléaniste . . ." He implies that Montfort came from a legitimist background.

Of the twenty ralliés that can be classified, eleven were Bonapartist, five Orleanist, two royalist. Of fifty-seven intransigents, twenty-six were legitimist, sixteen Bonapartist, ten Orleanist and five royalist of indeterminable hue. These figures warrant no more than the one generalization – about the legitimists. It may be possible to see in the Bonapartists two strains, a bourgeois longing for order and strong government that led to acceptance of the Republic, set off against those more boisterous spirits, represented by the quintet from Charente, who advocated a more popular democracy that the Republic of the Republicans, with whom they could not wish to deal. The intransigents were men of fervent political traditions, the ralliés had the same traditions but were more ready to compromise them for the preservation of the existing social order.

What made a deputy a rallié rather than an intransigent? In age, and length of previous parliamentary experience, the ralliés were younger. In occupation, the intransigents tended to be the ex-diplomats, the former administrative officials and the country gentlemen, the ralliés more the businessmen and industrialists. In political upbringing legitimism led to intransigence. Not surprisingly the old political traditions are easier to trace among the intransigents, a group of older men; but the ralliés by no means sprang from outside the traditional framework of the Right. When the catalogue of differences is exhausted, the chief impression is of similarity, in social terms, in education, in family background. Of the three groups that promoted the Ralliement, the Christian Democrats were meagrely represented by the abbés Gayraud and Lemire, the Social Catholics by de Mun, who linked them to the pious, submissive to the wishes of Leo XIII, and to the conservative politicians. These last controlled from 1893 to 1898 the fate of the Ralliement. No social barrier divided the two parliamentary groups; to pass from one to the other attitude was that much easier, but the ease was the same in both directions. With this in mind, it is time to examine their parliamentary record.

IV

In the Chamber that reassembled in November 1893 the Republican deputies for the first time could feel that the need for "concentration" had passed.

C'est parce que nous sommes ici, non plus 363, mais 488 députés républicains, c'est pour cela que nous voyons tomber et disparaître de lui-même, par la force des choses l'expédient, nécessairement provisoire, qui correspondait à la période des origines, de la lutte pour la vie, mais qui ne pouvait évidemment demeurer le régime normal et définitif du Gouvernement parlementaire en France.[24]

So Deschanel in the debate that brought down the Dupuy ministry. Millerand even before the elections had proclaimed the need to bury the slogan of Republican concentration, and had welcomed the prospect of a Republican conservative party that might help to break the political stalemate in the Republic of the Opportunists.[25]

The ralliés had not realized the high hopes of their election preparations. Of the groups of the traditional Right they represented only a third, thirty deputies out of eighty-six. But the parliamentary scene restored the effectiveness that the workings of the electoral system had seemed to deny the movement. For the Républicains de gouvernement amounted to between 250 and 300 deputies, at most a very bare majority of the Chamber, at worst a body flaking at either edge. No cabinet could rely solely on this centre force for a working majority; if the ralliés lived up to their promises, and still more if the whole of the Right followed their example, conservative government would become possible, the Radicals could be abandoned to flirt with the Socialists, and France would flourish under an avowed social conservatism. The *lois scolaires* might rest the sacred dogma, but their application would be tempered to the Catholicism of the right wing of the government coalition and to the desire of conservative Republicans to avoid vexation in public life.

Such was the support on which the Méline ministry was based from 1896 to 1898. Yet fully two and a half years passed before this stability was achieved. The study of the parliamentary action of the Right falls into two divisions: what was the role of the two groups in creating an opportunity for a cabinet such as Méline's, and how far did they go in supporting it? The absence of memoirs, the electoral defeat of the ralliés' only parliamentary strategist, Piou, and the lack of agreement among the intransigents leave the recorded votes of the deputies as the only sure guide to their behaviour. It was on their votes, moreover, that they were judged at the time by those conservative Republicans who

[24] November 23, 1893. *Journal officiel. Chambre. Débats parlementaires (J.O.)*, p. 106. The figure of 488 republicans presumably allows a round fifty each to the intransigent Right and to the Socialists.

[25] February 16, 1893. *J.O.*, p. 580.

were prepared, on certain terms, to reach agreement with them. The votes selected for study are those seven noted as significant for this period by André Siegfried[26] and a group of twelve, four of which coincide, used by A. Salles in the article previously mentioned to determine the political positions of the outgoing deputies of 1898;[27] to these votes have been added the one which brought down the Casimir-Périer government, and two in the spring of 1898.

The ministry formed by Casimir-Périer and presented to the Chamber on December 4, 1893, marked the shift in parliamentary attitudes. All its members had been elected as Républicains de gouvernement, and only one minister in the previous cabinet retained his post. As Minister of Public Worship in this government, Spuller, replying to a question from Denys Cochin on the obstructions placed by the Socialist mayor of St. Denis in the way of religious processions, called for "un esprit nouveau", an end to the petty persecution of religion. Brisson transformed the question into an interpellation, provoked Casimir-Périer into qualifying his minister's statement, but persisted in presenting an *ordre du jour* hostile to the government: "La Chambre, persistant dans les principes anti-cléricaux dont s'est toujours inspirée la politique républicaine et qui seuls peuvent préserver les droits de l'Etat laïque . . ." This was lost 197 to 291. The Chamber adopted by 280 to 120 the *ordre du jour* of Barthou and Lebon: "La Chambre, confiante dans la volonté du gouvernement pour maintenir les lois républicaines et défendre les droits de l'Etat laïque . . ." Both ralliés et intransigents could join in opposing Brisson; only Baudry d'Asson satisfied his hate of the Republic by supporting the *ordre du jour* Brisson. At the second vote the bulk of the ralliés supported the government, the intransigents abstained or voted with the opposition.[28]

The Right remained united, and in support of the government, when the Left moved for constitutional revision later in the month. The object of the resolution moved by Bourgeois (Jura) was the limitation of the Senate's powers. This found favour on the Right only in the

[26] A. Siegfried, *Tableau politique de la France de l'Ouest*, pp. 523-524. Two votes listed on p. 523, that of February 20, 1894, on a proposal for a wheat monopoly and that of February 21, 1894, on the 7 francs duty on wheat, have been omitted as not relevant to this study.

[27] A. Salles, "Les Députés sortants (1893-1898): Votes et Groupements", *Revue politique et parlementaire*, xvi (April 1898).

[28] March 3, 1894. *J.O.*, debate pp. 384-93, division lists pp. 395-6, 396-7. A. Siegfried, *op. cit.*, p. 523. A. Soulier, *L'Instabilité ministérielle sous la Troisième*

eyes of Brincard. Although constitutional revision was capable of leading some of the Right away from conciliation with the conservative Republicans, they had no wish to aid the Radicals by curtailing the role of the Senate.[29]

A more serious test of the intentions of the Right was the fall of the Casimir-Périer government. In May the Minister of Public Works, Jonnart, was attacked for denying to railway workers the right to form unions. The *ordre du jour pur et simple* was refused by 251 to 217 with 75 abstentions, the bulk of the ralliés voting for the government, the intransigents equally divided between support, opposition and abstention. The Right united could have saved the government, which on its desertion fell to an attack mounted by an intransigent, Ramel; by and large the ralliés had done their duty by a cabinet that had professed to meet their aims.[30]

Under the Dupuy cabinet there was a return to concentration in face of attacks from the extremes, Left and Right, such as had brought down Casimir-Périer. Even when Ribot had succeeded Dupuy at the head of a cabinet that marked a cautious step towards conservative government, the extreme Right had not learnt to accommodate itself to the inclina-

République (1939), pp. 418–9, gives a breakdown notably different from the following.

Ordre du jour Brisson:	FOR	AGAINST	ABSTAINED	ABSENT
Ralliés		27		3
Intransigents	1	47	2	4
Ordre du jour Barthou:	FOR	AGAINST	ABSTAINED	ABSENT
Ralliés	19	2	6	3
Intransigents	2	17	31	4

In the notes to this section the column heading underlined indicates the vote of Jules Méline.

[29] March 12–16, 1894. *J.O.*, debate pp. 492–507, 525–42, 550–62, division list pp. 570–1. A. Salles, op. cit., p. 38. The vote was taken on a motion to bury the resolution; the figures inverted, to read for and against revision are:

	FOR	AGAINST	ABSTAINED	ABSENT
Ralliés	1	23	2	5
Intransigents		49	1	4
Total	207	311	17	34

[30] May 22, 1894. *J.O.*, debate pp. 855–62, division list p. 867. A. Soulier, *op. cit.* p. 419, gives a breakdown that differs little.

	FOR	AGAINST	ABSTAINED	ABSENT
Ralliés	21	5	3	3
Intransigents	15	16	17	6

tions of the only body of Republican deputies with whom it could hope to work. In January 1895 Gauthier de Clagny moved for constitutional revision; in the only speech on the motion Goblet announced that he would support it despite his disapproval of the mover. The motion was lost 179 to 313 with 48 abstentions; the Right contributed 45 votes for the proposal and 13 of the abstentions. The proposal had no chance whatsoever of success. To vote for it could serve no purpose but to justify suspicions that the Right was not prepared to accept the Republic. This trap theralliés avoided far more successfully than the intransigents.[31]

Constitutional revision was one bogey of the Centre. The other was the income tax. Both were proposals that appeared to open the floodgates of revolution, the first by threatening the bulwark of stability, the Senate, the second by conjuring up visions of the redistribution of property. On the second issue the Right felt itself menaced as much as the Centre. The spring of 1896 was largely taken up by the efforts of the Bourgeois cabinet, France's first exclusively Radical government, to pass the income tax through the Chamber. Towards the end of March the Chamber adopted by 286 to 270 with 12 abstentions an *ordre du jour* proposed by Dron, which, for all its restrictive qualifying clauses, declared in principle for an income tax. This vote, on the face of it concerned with a fiscal principle, should be interpreted for the Republicans, as André Siegfried suggests, as on the continuance of the Bourgeois ministry. On either interpretation the Right, both intransigent and rallié, but for Sébastien Gavini, who was becoming more and more a Radical, was completely opposed.[32]

In the period before the formation of the Méline ministry the ralliés had largely justified their claims. They had supported religious appeasement and the government that had promised it most firmly; they had dissociated themselves from causes that no conservative Republican

[31] January 28, 1895. *J.O.*, debate pp. 82–3, division list pp. 86–7. A Salles, *op. cit.*, p. 38.

	FOR	AGAINST	ABSTAINED	ABSENT
Ralliés	8	13	7	6
Intransigents	37	4	6	7

[32] March 20–6, 1896. *J.O.*, debate on the 26th pp. 640–60, division list p. 665. A. Siegfried, *op. cit.* p. 523. A. Salles, *op. cit.*, pp. 38–9.

	FOR	AGAINST	ABSTAINED	ABSENT
Ralliés	1	31	1	1
Intransigents		52		1

would accept. The intransigents failed on three occasions to follow suit, on Barthou's *ordre du jour* that closed the debate in which Spuller called for "un esprit nouveau", on the fall of the Casimir-Périer cabinet, and on Gauthier de Clagny's motion for constitutional revision.

The Méline ministry depended on the votes of the Right at formation, in resisting the two most serious attacks on its general policy, and it fell despite the full support of the Right after the elections of 1898. Méline defeated two proposals for an income tax only with the votes of the Right, but on all the religious issues could have dispensed with their votes. By the end of the ministry's life the intransigents had virtually assumed the practice that the ralliés preached; yet even in 1898, admittedly when they could do so without endangering the government, the extremists could throw over the traces.

The Méline cabinet was immediately faced with an interpellation on the necessity of revising the constitution. Defeating an *ordre du jour* that reaffirmed the preponderance of universal suffrage, Méline secured by 278 to 244 with 16 abstentions the joining of approval of the ministerial statement to an affirmation of the sovereignty of universal suffrage. His Majority of thirty-four rested on the unequivocal support of both groups on the Right, of whom only the two Gavinis voted with the opposition.[33]

Two months later Méline called upon the same support to defeat Doumer's proposal of an income tax by a majority of twenty-nine. The voting was 254 in favour, with 26 abstentions. The whole of the Right voted against this Radical measure, with the exception of S. Gavini and Hugues, who supported it, and A. Gavini and Ornano, who abstained.[34]

The maintenance of the Concordat and the fulfilment of its provisions united not only the Right but so much of the Centre that the

[33] April 30, 1896. *J.O.*, debate pp. 751–66, division list pp. 769–70. A. Salles, *op. cit.*, p. 37.

	FOR	AGAINST	ABSTAINED	ABSENT
Ralliés	30	2	1	1
Intransigents	45		1	7

[34] July 6–7, 1896. *J.O.*, debate pp. 1213–21, 1223–38, division list pp. 1238–1239. Salles, *op. cit.*, p. 39.

	FOR	AGAINST	ABSTAINED	ABSENT
Ralliés	1	30	1	2
Intransigents	1	49	1	3

divisions would have been won by the government without the support of the Right. Two amendments proposed during the discussion of the budget for 1897 vented anticlerical emotions. The suppression of the French embassy at the Vatican was proposed by Hubbard, lost by 183 to 343 with 29 abstentions, and the suppression of the budget of Public Worship, moved by Fabérot, was lost by 178 to 338 with 35 abstentions. The latter proposal received twenty-six more votes than in 1895, when some Radicals had wished to avoid embarrassing the Bourgeois cabinet.[35]

Although Méline could muster a comfortable majority in debates on the public administration of religious affairs, anti-clericalism could be used to win back support for the tradition of Republican concentration. Delcassé took the opportunity of Berry's interpellation on the responsibilities for the fire at the Bazar de la Charité, to raise the old cry of Republican unity. Moved by the disaster, in which 117 people, many of them society ladies, lost their lives, the President of the Republic had attended the memorial service at Notre-Dame, the first official attendance at a religious ceremony since the passing of the law of August 14, 1884. At the service Father Ollivier, a Dominican, had preached a sermon in which the catastrophe was interpreted as a divine punishment of impious France. This thesis, propounded by a Dominican on an official occasion, might have been designed to raise protests. Brisson, President of the Chamber, had taken it upon himself to reply a few days later, but even a fortnight after this riposte Delcassé could threaten the government with a skilfully worded *ordre du jour*: "La Chambre, convaincue que seule une politique nouvelle, fondée sur l'union des républicains, peut rassurer le pays . . ." Priority was refused to this motion by a majority of 35, almost equalled by the 30 abstentions. The voting was 239 in favour, 274 against. S. Gavini sealed his conversion to

---

[35] On the Embassy: November 21, 1896. *J.O.*, debate pp. 1688–90, division list pp. 1696–7. A. Siegfried, *op. cit.*, p. 523. A. Salles, *op. cit.*, pp. 40–41.

	FOR	AGAINST	ABSTAINED	ABSENT
Ralliés		33		1
Intransigents		51	1	1

Budget of Public Worship: November 30, 1896. *J.O.*, debate pp. 1857–9 division list pp. 1866–7. A. Salles, *op. cit.*, p. 40.

	FOR	AGAINST	ABSTAINED	ABSENT
Ralliés		33		1
Intransigents		49		5

Radicalism by voting for the priority of Delcassé's *ordre du jour*. But Méline had been saved by the Right.[36]

As July came round a proposal for an income tax raised a head that was to become hoary before enactment. Although the scheme had lost ground in the Chamber by five votes since it had been moved in the previous year, the Right remained essential if Méline was to preserve the nation from so terrifying an innovation. The Right did not fail him.[37]

During the winter the Radicals went through the ritual prescribed by anticlericalism. Dubief and others invited the government to take "les mesures nécessaires pour que la laïcisation soit partout achevée dans le delai de dix ans", a suggestion that received eight votes less than a similar motion in the previous year, 216 to the government's 312 and 20 abstentions. Denunciation of the Concordat was even less popular; the thoroughgoing anticlericals were 183 against 311 and 49 abstentions. The Right made good its claim to be the champion of the Church, but its support was on these occasions superfluous.[38]

[36] A. Dansette, *Histoire religieuse de la France contemporaine*, ii, 250–1, and A. Debidour, *L'Eglise catholique et l'Etat sous la Troisième République* (1909) ii, 159–61, give accounts of the affair. On the debate on May 29, 1897: *J.O.*, debate pp. 1323–37, division list pp. 1338–9. A. Siegfried, *op. cit.*, p. 523. A. Salles, *op. cit.*, pp. 37–8.

	FOR	AGAINST	ABSTAINED	ABSENT
Ralliés	1	31		3
Intransigents		50	3	

[37] July 16, 1897. *J.O.*, debate pp. 1996–2014, division list pp. 2016–7. A. Salles, *op. cit.*, p. 40.

	FOR	AGAINST	ABSTAINED	ABSENT
Ralliés	1	32	1	1
Intransigents		49	1	4
Total	249	282	23	23

[38] Laïcisation: November 29, 1897. *J.O.*, debate pp. 2636–42, division list pp. 2646–7. A. Salles, *op. cit.*, p. 41.

	FOR	AGAINST	ABSTAINED	ABSENT
Ralliés		35		1
Intransigents		51		2

Denunciation of Concordat: January 21, 1898. *J.O.*, debate pp. 146–7, division list pp. 150–1. A. Salles, *op. cit.*, p. 40.

	FOR	AGAINST	ABSTAINED	ABSENT
Ralliés		34		2
Intransigents		51	1	1

In the spring of 1898 the Left opened the last full-dress debate before the elections on the general conduct of the government. The speakers for the opposition were Millerand, Bourgeois and Dron, who proposed the following *ordre du jour*: "La Chambre invite le Gouvernement à reprendre la politique traditionnelle du parti républicain . . ." Denys Cochin spoke for the Right that was not committed to the Republic in language that sounds anachronistic after two years of the Méline ministry:

> En somme à propos de la prétendue alliance [between Méline and the Right], M. le président du conseil disait: Nous n'avons rien promis, parce que nous ne pouvons pas renoncer à nos principes fondamentaux.
> Je retourne le mot . . .

The grudging tone was not redeemed by the earlier statement by Denys Cochin that

> Nous usons et continuerons à user de notre droit et à faire œuvre de bon sens en appuyant de nos votes ceux qui se rapprochent le plus de nos idées.

The reaction of both groups on the Right showed traces of the cleavage that had divided them in the 1893 elections. In each group a deputy voted against the ministry; by 1898 S. Gavini can scarcely be classed as a rallié, while Largentaye was still indulging in the luxury of an outmoded tactic. The significant variation was in the abstention of ten of the intransigents. Even if Méline scarcely needed the votes of the Right to carry a motion of confidence by 295 to 213, this was no encouragement to those who dreamed of a Tory party on the English model.[39]

Two days later the comte de Lanjuinais rose to explain why he and certain of his friends would not vote for the general budget resolution. He briefly traced the arguments that had been used by the Right to oppose taxes levied on the capital of the religious orders, before turning to attack the "electoral pillage" of France. But he had chosen to put first an issue that the Catholic hierarchy had never wished to press

---

[39] March 12, 1898. *J.O.*, debate pp. 1205–34, division list pp. 1235–6. A. Siegfried, *op. cit.*, p. 523. A. Salles, *op. cit.*, p. 37.

	FOR	AGAINST	ABSTAINED	ABSENT
Ralliés	32	1		2
Intransigents	39	1	10	4

with undue force, and which had been effectively settled by the passage of time. Lanjuinais was followed by twenty-three intransigents and three ralliés, the latter being Dupuytrem, Gayraud and Montalembert. The budget was passed by 450 to 31. Nevertheless the Ralliement as a parliamentary system had owed its success to the tacit understanding that religious affairs were better not ventilated in the Chamber. The Radicals had tried to disrupt the government's support by tactics designed to wear down both edges of the conservative block; there seemed no reason for them to despair of ultimate success.[40]

The final achievement of the extreme Right in the Chamber of 1893–8 was to recreate Republican concentration on a constitutional issue by supporting Guesde's proposal that candidates should be once more allowed to stand in more than one constituency simultaneously. Until the near-disaster of 1885 this had been a good Republican measure. Discredited in the eyes of the Centre by the use made of it by Boulanger, it was now cherished only by the extremes. In March 1898 Guesde could muster only 134 votes, 47 from the Right, to the government's 349. The intransigents voted heavily in favour of this revision, that could no longer bring them any advantage, while the ralliés divided uneasily, with the majority on the side of reason.[41]

The duration of the Méline ministry, from April 1896 to June 1898, was the greatest that had so far been allowed under the Third Republic. This alone was a considerable tribute to the parliamentary success of the Ralliement. From 1896 onwards even the most intransigent of the Right had voted in cases of need for a conservative Republican government. Yet, as the last three divisions analysed show, there were still many intransigent deputies ready to vote, on less vital occasions, for motions repugnant to conservative Republicans. A parliamentary strategy of rapprochement with the Republican Right had won an uneasy acceptance.

[40] March 14, 1898. *J.O.*, debate: Lanjuinais pp. 1276–7; division list pp. 1290–1.

	FOR	AGAINST	ABSTAINED	ABSENT
Ralliés	29		3	2
Intransigents	20		23	10

[41] March 28, 1898. *J.O.*, debate pp. 1426–34, division list pp. 1438–9.

	FOR	AGAINST	ABSTAINED	ABSENT
Ralliés	9	18	3	4
Intransigents	38	7	1	7

That it had been accepted is perhaps shown by the actions of those deputies of the Right in the 1893-8 Chamber who survived the elections, thirty-five intransigents and twenty-seven ralliés. As soon as the Chamber reassembled the Radicals and Socialists challenged the government in a two-day debate closed by a confused series of votes on the *ordre du jour*. The two crucial votes were the government's carrying, by 295 to 272, of the first phrase of Ribot's motion "La Chambre approuvant les déclarations du Gouvernement . . .", and the passing, by 295 to 246 against Méline's opposition, of Ricard's addition ". . . et appuyée sur une majorité exclusivement républicaine . . ." In the first of these votes Baudry d'Asson and Largentaye opposed Méline, in the second Largentaye and Pontbriand abstained. With these exceptions the survivors of the Right in the previous legislature voted solidly for Méline. But it was of no avail. The parliamentary situation had been changed by the general elections, and the reasons for this change are to be sought outside the Chamber.[42]

V

The fall of Méline stemmed from electoral defeat, a defeat that was in large part caused by the lack of co-ordination between the Right in the Chamber and their followers in the constituencies. In the Chamber the Ralliement was a neat, definable parliamentary strategy, based on a tacit agreement between the Right and the Republican conservatives. The problem was to reflect that agreement, contrary as it was to French political life in the late nineteenth century, in the electoral struggles throughout the country.

Barthou's conduct of the elections as Minister of the Interior has been much criticized. Accused on the Left of exerting too much administrative pressure against the Radicals and their allies, on the Right of attacking their deputies however loyally they had supported Méline, he appears an ambiguous figure. Two printed sources exist that give accounts of the negotiations between Méline and the Right before and during the 1898 elections: Piou, the Catholic politician, and Lachapelle,

[42] The debate was on June 13-14, 1898. *J.O.*, debate pp. 1760-74, 1777-93; division list pp. 1795-6 (first phrase) and p. 1797 (addition Ricard). A. Siegfried, *op. cit.*, pp. 523-4. On the parliamentary tactics: A. Soulier, *op. cit.*, pp. 139-40. For an analysis of the voting: G. Lachapelle, *Le Ministère Méline* (1928), pp. 200-2.

the "official" historian of the Méline ministry, agree on the cause of the negotiations failure.[43]

The Vatican had been much preoccupied by the approaching elections and was determined that the Right should fight as loyal Republicans. To this end it had exerted its influence to place at the head of the electoral committee Etienne Lamy, a Catholic *littérateur*, contributor to the *Revue des Deux Mondes*, a man of an unimpeachably Republican past since he had been one of the 363 deputies who voted defiance to MacMahon. Lamy had an interview with Méline shortly before the election,[44] at which Lamy demanded that candidates who expected Catholic votes should formally promise the revision of the "lois scolaire et militaire". Méline offered that the Progressistes should maintain a discreet silence on this issue, to which Lamy replied with a *non possumus*.[45] Relations were closed on this note of intransigence until after the first ballot, at which the Left made notable gains. Lamy at this point retired into the background,[46] leaving Piou to salvage what was possible. Piou saw Méline,[47] and reached agreement for the second ballot, not on a programme but on a list of names. It is hard not to agree with Lachapelle that the truth of the matter was that the parliamentary Right had had nothing to do with the organization of the campaign launched in the constituencies against the conservative Republicans, but that it had not dared to disavow it.

The mismanagement of the Right's electoral campaign was partly the consequence of the disunity among the supporters of the Ralliement. Of the three groups, the straightforwardly conservative, the Social Catholics and the Christian Democrats, it was the conservatives who were the bulk of the deputies; indeed, for all their actual support of Méline in the lobbies, many deputies were still in 1898 formally on record as opposing the Ralliement. The Vatican therefore tried to take the control of the election preparations out of their hands. Unfortunately power was given to clerics who were far less pliant in political

[43] J. Piou, *Le Ralliement*, pp. 73–8. G. Lachapelle, *Le Ministère Méline*, pp. 173–81; see the Foreword for the official character of this work, read and altered by Méline. Dansette, *Histoire religieuse de la France contemporaine*, ii (see p. 665), had access to Lamy's papers on the preparations for the elections; his account (p. 259) of the elections appears to draw nothing from them.

[44] Piou, p. 74. Lachapelle, p. 178 n.

[45] Piou, pp. 74–5, and implied by Lachapelle, p. 178 n.

[46] R. Cornilleau, *Le Ralliement a-t-il échoué?* (1927), p. 38.

[47] On this Piou, pp. 76–7, is the sole source, save for a more discreet account in Cornilleau, p. 38.

negotiation, and to Lamy who attached an undue importance to the form of words and lacked the judgement to accept the results that might flow from tacit understanding.

The activities of Lamy would alone account for the difficulties of organizing an effective electoral pact between the Catholic Right and the conservative Republicans. But a survey of departmental politics, necessarily incomplete because the monographs are as yet few, reveals the gulf between Paris and the provinces. The Chamber may have been sovereign in the Third Republic in that its actions seemed more independent of the electorate than in other democracies; the corollary was also true, that politics in the departments led a life that was not always easy to influence from Paris, as Méline, Lamy and Piou all found to their cost.

In Côte d'Or[48] the Ralliement made little difference to the behaviour of the Catholic voters. In 1889 there had been five Catholic conservatives in the field; at Semur, the only constituency in which the Catholic had retired before the second ballot, his electors followed his exhortation to practise the *politique du pire* and helped to elect a Radical against a moderate. In 1893 there was only one avowed Catholic, at Beaune II; elsewhere the voters of the Right seemed to have stayed away, except perhaps at Dijon I where the Republican *le Progrès de la Côte-d'Or* claimed that the victorious Socialist had received 1,500 Catholic votes, a claim denied by the Catholic *le Bien Public*. In 1898 there were six rallié candidates, two of whom retired before the second ballot; the votes of one went almost entirely to the moderate, but at Châtillon the Catholics appear to have favoured the moderate Leroy less than his Radical opponent.[49] At Beaune II where the moderate retired, his voters favoured the Radical more than the rallié. At Dijon I the Socialist Vaux was re-elected for lack of agreement among his opponents. The Ralliement had amounted to a few fairer words.

In Basses-Pyrénées[50] the traditional conservatism was killed in the 1890's, replaced by Republican social conservatism. In 1889 there had been candidates of the Right in six of the seven constituencies, of whom two had been elected, in 1893 four candidates, none elected, in 1898 not a single candidate. The most interesting contest was Bayonne II in 1893, in which Harriague defeated an intransigent priest, Mgr.

[48] R. Long, *Les Elections législatives en Côte-d'Or* (1958), pp. 70–90.
[49] Leroy was one of the fifty deputies whose defection on June 14, 1898, brought Méline down.
[50] René Cuzacq, *Elections législatives à Bayonne*, Vol. II (Bayonne, 1951).

Diharassary. Harriague, rich, "of a religious frame of mind", was supported by the young duc de Grammont, who had considered standing as a rallié but withdrawn for lack of Republican support and in face of a whispering campaign that he wanted a diplomatic post. A campaign against "the domination of the clergy" was launched against Diharassary, who was backed by most of the priests in spite of the disapproval of his bishop, an ambitious prelate anxious to find favour with the rulers of the Republic. By 1898 the department had realized that the Republican conservatives were quite satisfactory conservatives.

In Ardèche[51] in 1893 Vogüé had been urged to stand by a group that included Jules Roche, a former Republican minister. The opposition to him was festering on the Right: he had married a "schismatic" – his wife was Russian; he had expressed liberal opinions in his book on a journey to Palestine; Renan was his colleague at the Academy. But for the candidature of Le Roy, an even less agreeable Republican, Vogüé might well have had a royalist opponent. As it was he inherited the voters of the Right and won. In 1898 Jules Roche increased the majority over Le Roy with fierce denunciation of Republican concentration. In this constituency, Tournon II, the Ralliement had succeeded.

In Tarn[52] also, successes had been achieved: the Reille dynasty had responded to the Pope's wishes, and in Tarn the Reilles were the Right. From 1876 to 1958, with a break from 1924 to 1928, a Reille has been deputy for Tarn; between 1894 and 1910 there were two, not to mention Solages, a son-in-law of baron René Reille, who sat from 1889 to 1892 and was re-elected in 1898, defeating Jaurès. This was a case of the voters following the inclinations of a family. The opposite was true in Hautes-Pyrénées[53] in which Fould felt it necessary to become less and less conservative in order to retain votes, while Alicot, a conservative Republican, at last was able to obtain conservative support previously denied to him.

In Brest III[54] in 1897 the intransigents and the ralliés fought a des-

[51] A. Siegfried, *Géographie électorale de l'Ardèche* (1949), pp. 85–7, 125–6. But more can be found in the report of the parliamentary enquiry into Vogüé's election: *Impressions parlementaires. Chambre. 6e législature*, Vol. VI, no. 407 (annexe au procès verbal . . . 20 février 1894).

[52] Pierre Doueil, *Geographie électorale du Tarn* (unpublished thesis, Castres, 1953).

[53] Philippe Peltier, *Politique et psychologie rurales dans les Hautes-Pyrénées depuis 1871* (Unpublished thesis, Institut d'Etudes Politiques, Paris, 1957).

[54] A. Siegfried, *Tableau politique de la France de l'Ouest*, pp. 181–94. The report of the parliamentary commission of enquiry is *Impressions parlementaires. Chambre. 6e législature*, Vol. 47, No. 2451 (annexe au procès-verbal de la séance du 24 mai 1897).

perate battle long after both groups of the Right in the Chamber had adopted the same strategy. Local jealousy between the priests and the nobility was partly responsible. One man's thwarted ambition played a role: the comte de Blois, the intransigent candidate, having twice failed to obtain the Catholic electoral committee's nomination against distinguished prelates, (in 1880 Freppel, Bishop of Angers, in 1892 Mgr. d'Hulst), now felt that he could defeat the candidate of the priests of Léon. The struggle was waged with many of the usual weapons; it was alleged that money was distributed, drinks freely given, women intimidated. The priests, so their opponents claimed, had made every possible use of their position to further the cause of the abbé Gayraud; they had preached sermons in his favour, refused absolution to supporters of the comte de Blois, encouraged seminarists to write to relatives and had threatened recalcitrant parishioners with the expulsion of their daughters from religious orders. The nobility, it was retorted, had used threats of eviction. A parliamentary commission, composed entirely of Republicans, sat gaping while the evidence was given, and recommended the invalidation of Gayraud, who was promptly re-elected with an increased majority. It was all very different from what went on in the Palais-Bourbon.

Among the reasons for the fall of Méline the chief was the ill-success of the Right's electoral campaign. The first vote in the new Chamber showed that the opposition to Méline could muster 272 deputies, nearly twenty more than on any major issue in the last two years of the old Chamber. Lachapelle suggests that thirty nationalists had been elected on the votes of the Right; promoters of the Ralliement accepted the estimate of the *Journal de Roubaix* that 62 "sectaires" had been elected because Catholics practised the *politique du pire*.[55] Even so the government majority on the first vote was 23; defeat came when on the second vote 21 previous supporters abstained and 30 deserted to the opposition, many of them in revenge for electoral opposition from the Right.[56]

Three factors were at play. While both right-wing and Republican deputies could be won over to co-operation, their electors were much

[55] G. Lachapelle, *Le Ministère Méline*, p. 200; P. Dabry, *Les Catholiques républicains, 1890–1903* (1905) pp. 575 ff.

[56] G. Lachapelle, *op. cit.*, p. 201, lists 40, of whom five are cited in his survey of the election, pp. 177–8. Of the 51, ten were from Nord, five from Dordogne, three from Gironde and four from Savoie.

less willing to give up stereotyped political attitudes. In this the Catholic voters of Côte-d'Or were typical; in the same department Spuller, whom it elected to the Senate in 1893, found a cool welcome among his supporters when he called for "un esprit nouveau".[57] Secondly, Lamy's conduct of the pre-electoral negotiations destroyed any hope of reaching agreement with the conservative Republicans, in alliance with whom the Right should have fought the elections. Finally, it may be doubted whether any such agreement when made would have been loyally accepted by the whole of the Right. The discord fomented by the polemics of the Catholic press, the clash of personalities, were such as to hamper an attempt to impose unity of electoral strategy, especially under the well-meaning but ineffectual leadership of Lamy. For none of the deputies of the Right carried the weight of Paul de Cassagnac in *l'Autorité*, of Father Bailly in *la Croix* or of Drumont in *la Libre Parole*. It was the misfortune of the Ralliement that the three stars of the Catholic press should have been intransigents.

It was the parliamentary Right, however, that had made possible the transitory achievements of 1893–1898. The Ralliement offered these deputies a chance to clothe their conservatism in a more modern garb. By doing so the traditional Right prolonged its life. If union with the conservative Republicans had proved impossible, at least for two years a new framework had been imposed on politics in the Chamber. The Ralliement had demonstrated that Republican concentration was no longer the only viable majority.

[57] See the memorial volume on Spuller, published anonymously at Evreux in 1903—in the Bibliothèque Nationale: 8⁰ Ln²⁷. 49585.

© DAVID SHAPIRO 1962

THE NATIONALIST MOVEMENT
IN PARIS, 1900–1906

By D. R. Watson

I

FROM THE TIME of the Dreyfus Affair to the collapse of the Third Republic in 1940 nationalism was almost exclusively invoked by the Right in French politics. In the period 1914–40 the word national in the title of a political formation was almost certainly a sign that it was of the Right; while a "National" government signified a coalition of the Right and the Centre as surely as the stressing of "republican" meant a coalition of Left and Centre. But this had not always been the case. During the revolution "patriot" had been another term for revolutionary, as it had denoted the radicals in eighteenth-century England and America; and from 1815 to 1848 it was the opposition of the Left that appealed to the feelings of national pride. For the remainder of the century nationalism was politically neutral; it was stressed or rejected by both sides according to the needs of the moment. In reaction to the nationalistic policy of Louis Napoleon the opposition of the Left became for a time almost pacifist.[1] The events of 1870 saw an abrupt reversal, with the attempt to revive the patriotic and revolutionary ardour of 1792. The revolt of the Commune of Paris was the most violent expression of this mixture of patriotic fervour and class warfare. The double defeat of both the regular imperial troops and of the Republican militia disillusioned both conservatives and radicals, and plunged France into a period of dejection. But until the Boulangist crisis desire to avenge the defeat of 1870 was expressed most strongly by the Left.

The purpose of this essay is to examine the growth of a new nationalist feeling after the Dreyfus Affair, which became an important new element in the Right. It was partly this adoption of nationalism that

[1] R. Girardet, *La Société militaire dans la France contemporaine* (1953), p. 194.

was responsible for the survival of important numbers of the Right; for if there is a remarkable continuity between the 45 per cent of the electorate that voted against the Republic in 1877 and the 44½ per cent that voted for the *Poincaristes* in 1928, it was certainly not the same areas or the same social conditions that made up the troops of the Right on these two occasions.[2] As Nord, which in spite of industrialization had at first been retained for the Right by its Catholicism, moved over to the Left, it was replaced by the districts close to the German frontier on the northeast, which had been on the Left in the first days of the Republic, but which were won over to the Right by nationalism. A similar phenomenon, but one that is not so readily located geographically, is the swing of certain social classes from the parties of the Left to those of the Right.

One of these changes was the process by which Paris passed from the control of an alliance of Radicals and Socialists into the hands of the Right. In the nineteenth century Paris had always been in the control of the Left. After the Nationalist victories in the elections of 1900 and 1902 it has remained on the whole in the hands of the Right. It was not simply that the electorate of the city was always chauvinistic, and passed from the Jacobin nationalism of the Republicans to the nationalism of the anti-Dreyfusards. The process was more complicated, as is shown by the contrasts between the reactions of areas of different social composition.

The change was partly due to population movements. At the present day the central areas of Paris (those included in the first 10 arrondissements) are much wealthier than the outer ring (made up of arrondissements 11 to 20) and the suburbs beyond the city itself. These are mainly industrial and poor residential areas; it is only beyond them again that the wealthy suburbs begin. This contrast between the central areas and the outer ring of poverty was already clearly defined in 1890 when Dr. J. Bertillon, head of the statistical section of the Prefecture, produced a demographic survey of the city based on the statistics provided by the census. It probably goes back to the period 1860–85 when most of the modern city was created. It was then that many (though by no means all) of the old tenements of the central areas were pulled down to be replaced by new blocks, that had supplies of gas and water, and the new standards of comfort demanded by the bourgeoisie. The rents for these new flats were too high for the poorer inhabitants and they

[2] F. Goguel, *La Politique des partis sous la Troisième République* (Foreword to the 2nd edition, 1958), p. 20.

PARIS
The quartiers and arrondissements

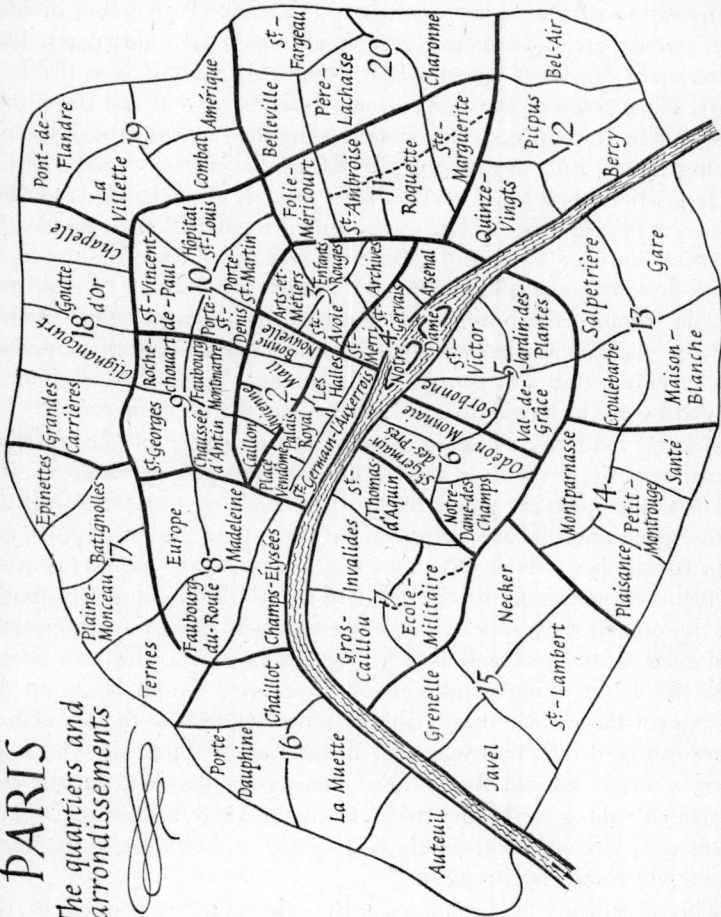

had to move out into the outer areas, up to that time half-built, and now covered with cheap blocks of flats.

Bertillon's volume, entitled *Résultats statistiques du dénombrement de 1891 pour la ville de Paris*, is the basis of any classification of the social composition of the eighty quartiers of the city (Paris being divided into twenty arrondissements, each made up of four quartiers). Unfortunately the latest occasion for which this analysis is available is 1891. Later censuses were taken on a different system and the results prepared by the national office instead of by the Prefecture of the Seine, giving figures only as averages for the whole of Paris, instead of for each quartier; but it seems very unlikely that any areas changed radically between 1891 and 1900. The method used by Bertillon to divide the quartiers into six degrees of prosperity was to combine the results of the following series obtained by the census: the number of male and female servants, the number of contracts of marriage (which would only be made by spouses who had a considerable amount of property), the average number of people per room, and the number of children helped by the local welfare committees (*bureaux de bienfaisance*).

Another and distinct indication of the character of the different quartiers is the division of the population into *patrons, employés,* and *ouvriers*. The quartiers where the workers made up more than half the active population include all those classed as poor and very poor, except Batignolles (which was a mixed area between the wealthy districts of Plaine Monceau on the one side and the northern industrial suburbs on the other); they also include eight quartiers classed as prosperous, and even Monnaie classed as rich. The explanation is that in a mixed area the better living conditions of a minority would bring up the average of the whole quartier although the majority of the population were not well off. This was clear in the case of Monnaie where the narrow streets around Buci housed many poor families, but the rich apartments along the Boulevard St. Germain raised the average figures. Most quartiers were sufficiently homogeneous, however, to be fairly accurately placed by Bertillon.

This classification is supported by other figures printed in the *Annuaire Statistique de la Ville de Paris*. The details vary, but the general picture is the same; a compact western area where infant mortality and deaths from T.B. are low, and where there is little overcrowding, surrounded by an intermediate zone, and finally around the edge of the city an area with high death rates and unsatisfactory housing conditions. These social divisions are followed closely by contrasts in religious observance as measured by the proportion of civil funerals. The prosperous areas have very few civil funerals, the poor areas a very much higher number. The atheism of the 20th arrondissement, where 38 per cent of funerals were civil, is very striking, even when compared with surrounding areas where the Church would seem to have been equally out of touch with the population. For the largest parish in Paris was in the 18th not the 20th arrondissement.[3]

This classification reveals at once that the poor and very poor quartiers form a compact belt running round the outer edge of the city in a vast U-shape with its open end in the west, where the rich residential areas of the 16th arrondissement meet the Bois de Boulogne. Commencing in the quartier of Batignolles in the 17th arrondissement the poor districts run along the northern slopes of the hill of Montmartre through the industrial areas around the great railway yards of the Gare du Nord and Gare de l'Est: turning south they include the unsavoury area of La Villette where were concentrated the slaughterhouse, gasworks and the docks at the end of the canals coming from the east, and run south in a broad belt to the Seine with the single exception of the Bel Air quartier. Across the river through the 13th, 14th and 15th arrondissements the poor areas stretch out westwards.

Within the centre of the U it is again true that from a focus on the Champs-Elysées wealth spreads out in diminishing intensity. With three exceptions the prosperous quartiers are clustered in the eastern area at the base of the U, leaving a compact group of rich quartiers centred on the 7th and 8th arrondissements.

This essay then describes the Nationalist campaign that led to the swing of Paris from the Left to the Right, and compares the electoral success of the Nationalist candidates with the social conditions of the different areas. This comparison is important because the Nationalists, in order to exaggerate their success (for Paris was the area where they had the greatest electoral success), talked as if they had been supported unanimously by the voters of the capital. In fact their success was very limited outside the prosperous areas, and when their votes are compared with those cast in previous elections, it can be seen that they were building on conservative elements that already existed. They extended them a little, and swung the balance of power in the municipal council by joining with the old Right which had before been isolated. But their victory was by no means the tidal wave which they claimed.

The main sources used, apart from the demographic material

[3] Y. Daniel, *Equipement paroissial d'un diocèse urbain* (1956), p. 169.

described above, are, first, the results of the municipal elections of 1896, 1900, and 1904, and of the legislative elections of 1898, 1902, and 1906, from the official returns in the Archives of the department of Seine. Information about the electoral campaigns is provided by the material collected from the enquiries into disputed elections by the committees of the Chamber, which is to be found in the Archives Nationales for the 1898 elections, and in the archives of the Assemblée Nationale for 1902 and 1906. A much larger collection of electoral propaganda, posters, and pamphlets covering both municipal and legislative elections, is preserved in the Bibliothèque Historique de la Ville de Paris. Finally the local newspapers produced weekly in the different constituencies by nearly all serious candidates, some only during the few weeks of the campaign, but others continuing for several years, provide a wealth of information about the themes of the electoral battle.

New political issues ended the rule of the Radicals, who had controlled the municipal council and dominated the representation of Paris at the Palais Bourbon since 1880. The Left had their most complete victory in 1893 when the anti-republican Right was discredited by Boulangism, and the opportunist Republicans were discredited by the Panama scandals. Even the *bien pensant* 7th arrondissement had a Radical deputy as a result of conflict between the Boulangists and the supporters of Cochin, a monarchist who refused to join the Boulangist coalition.

But this victory was the first step towards the end of the Radical rule in Paris. For it meant the emergence of a group of Socialist deputies, and encouraged the coming together of Opportunists and the Right proper in the Ralliement. Radicals and Socialists continued to work together in the campaign against the Presidency of Casimir-Périer and for the municipal elections of 1896. This was another victory for the Left, and led to Millerand's formulation of the programme of "Collectivist Socialism" at the banquet of St. Mandé, and to the formation of a strong Socialist group at the Hôtel de Ville. In 1898 they were able to insist that the Radicals shared the Presidency of the municipal council with them in alternate years.

It was in these circumstances that the Dreyfus Affair led to a crystallisation of political conflicts. The majority of the municipal council was Dreyfusard from December 1898. A by-election in 1899 led to the election of the first anti-Dreyfusard Nationalist in the commercial area of the 10th arrondissement which had been a Radical stronghold.

In 1900 and 1902 the Nationalists, organised by the Ligue de la Patrie

Française, but including members of the Ligue des Patriotes and other groups, won a third of the votes of Paris, and were able to swing the municipal council from Left to Right. This essay describes the foundation of the Patrie Française, outlines its programme, and compares the Nationalist vote with the social composition of the different quartiers of the city.

The concluding sections deal with the break-up of the Patrie Française and the absence of an organised Nationalist campaign in the elections of 1904 and 1906, and the circumstances in which the municipal council, which had been won back by the coalition of Radicals and Socialists in 1904, was finally won by the Right.

II

The elections of 1893, when Paris seemed to be one of the most "advanced" areas in France, proved to be the apogee of the Left. Only four out of thirty-three deputies elected in 1893 were of the Right, representing the wealthy areas of the 8th and 9th arrondissements. The only slightly less rich residential areas of the 7th and 16th arrondissements were represented by Radicals as were the commercial constituencies of central Paris, the 1st, 2nd, and 3rd arrondissements. The Radicals had twelve deputies, the Socialists seventeen, soon joined by four who had been elected as Boulangists. Socialists and Boulangists together represented almost the whole of the U-shaped belt of poor and very poor quartiers that ringed Paris. The only exceptions were two Radicals, Jacques and Lockroy. Socialists also held the two seats of the 5th arrondissement which Bertillon classed as prosperous. But it must be remembered that these party titles were only vague statements of faith, not precise descriptions of affiliation to organized parties. Marcel Prélot points out that at this time the word socialist was in danger of becoming a mere "manner of hoping in common"; it was to fix the frontiers of Socialist doctrine that Millerand in 1896 made his famous speech at St. Mandé.[4] The Guesdiste group, by far the most disciplined and organised of all the Socialist factions, had almost no support in Paris, where Socialism was the continuation of the revolutionary and radical tradition of opposition to established authority, with the Commune as its most vital memory. The Radicals were even less of an organised group than the Socialists; there were many like the

[4] M. Prélot, *L'Evolution politique du socialisme français* (1939), p. 111.

Radical described in the report of the Prefect of the Seine to Waldeck-Rousseau as Minister of the Interior:

> Si M. Vaudet qui s'intitule Radical-Socialiste croit trouver quelques chances de succès en modérant son programme il ne hésitera pas à le faire.[5]

The municipal council was just as firmly in the hands of the Left as the Parliamentary representation of Paris. After the elections of 1896 the Radical group called "Les Droits de Paris" numbered thirty-three and were in permanent alliance with nineteen councillors who professed different shades of socialism, ranging from vague Republican socialism, through the followers of Brousse, who hoped for complete state control of the economy but rejected violent political change, to Blanquists and Allemanistes, who proclaimed that the hour was near when the workers would rise to destroy their oppressors. Together the Radicals and Socialists numbered fifty-two out of a council of eighty, and thus had a secure majority.[6] This was to be the highwater mark of the electoral success of the Left in Paris.

The Ralliement is important in Paris because it began that movement to the Right which was to be given such a powerful stimulus by the nationalism of the Dreyfus Affair. As long as the main political conflict was about the regime Paris was firmly on the Left. But this was only because the Left was an alliance of Republicans and Socialists that had opposed views about a second set of questions. The alliance was not only between elected representatives, where Republicans and Socialists joined together to control the municipal council, but also among the electorate; the majorities of most candidates of the Left were made up of the same coalition, against the extremes of reaction and collectivism. Thus their electoral campaigns talked of measures of reform to satisfy the more radical part of their electorate, while insisting on caution and legality so as not to offend the conservative. The Ralliement began to break up this coalition of the Centre, by detaching some voters to the Right. Nationalism continued the process by winning more voters for the Right, and attaching the others more firmly to the Left.

[5] Institut de France, Waldeck-Rousseau Papers, MSS 4577 (1) (with reference to the municipal elections of 1900).

[6] The name of the Radical group was derived from the Ligue d'union républicaine des droits de Paris, founded on April 3, 1871 by Clemenceau, Lockroy, Floquet, and Alain-Targé to mediate between the *communards* and the government at Versailles.

The Parliamentary elections of 1898 marked this swing to the Right. Four Radicals were defeated and replaced by five conservatives.[7] But the Radicals made up for this loss in the prosperous areas by defeating three Socialists and one Boulangist in the popular areas. This left Paris represented by sixteen Socialists, eleven Radicals and ten conservatives of varying persuasions. The only change in favour of the Left was that Girou (a former Boulangist) stood as a Socialist and defeated the Radical Jacques in the 14th arrondissement.

But the by-elections to the muncipal council did not reflect this trend. In the twenty-two by-elections between 1896 and 1900, five Radicals were replaced by Socialists and four conservatives by Radicals; in only three cases were the changes from Left to Right. The explanation is that in municipal elections even more than in legislative ones the person of the candidate was more important than his political label. As the *maire* of the 13th arrondissement reported to the Prefect,

"Here it depends more on the individual than on his politics." [8]

And it was quite likely that the next most important local politician who would move into the council when the councillor became a deputy, would in previous campaigns have adopted a political position to the Left of the occupier of the fief. For he would have won his position by campaigning against the sitting councillor. For example Mill, who in 1896 stood as a Radical against Riant (a member of the conservative group Républicains Municipaux) was badly beaten; in 1898, on Riant's death, Mill again stood and was elected as a Radical.

This was the situation in Paris when the nationalist campaign began. In order to make this intelligible it is necessary to refer briefly to the development of the Dreyfus Affair. Dreyfus had been condemned in 1894 and had disappeared from public view to the torments of his confinement on Devil's Island. The first statement of Dreyfus' innocence was Bernard Lazare's pamphlet which appeared in November 1896; Scheurer-Kestner, the vice-president of the Senate, began working for revision of the case behind the scenes in the next year, but it was November 1897 before Dreyfus' brother denounced Esterhazy and the

[7] The 16th arrondissement had been divided into two constituencies. Throughout the essay "conservative" stands for all political tendencies except Radicals, Socialists and Nationalists: it includes Royalists, Bonapartists, Ralliés, and Républicains Modérés or Progressistes.

[8] Archives Départementales de la Seine, file of election literature (letter of April 21, 1902).

case really became a public quarrel. The acquittal of Esterhazy in January 1898, followed by Zola's open letter "J'accuse" and his own trial in February first convinced a large mass of people that justice had not been done. The Ligue des Droits de l'Homme was refounded in February 1898. But the affair was still in a legal rather than a political stage, as the prime minister Méline refused to take up a position. The elections of April 1898 were hardly affected by the Affair.[9]

But for the next two years the Affair was to occupy the political stage to the exclusion of almost everything else. The exacerbation of the Affair was partly due to the incoherence of the Chamber produced by the 1898 elections. The union of the conservative Republicans and ralliés that had supported Méline failed to carry the country; on the other hand, as the opposition to Méline consisted of the extreme Right and extreme Left there was no alternative majority to take his place. Brisson, who was called upon to form a Radical cabinet determined to win the support of the small group of nationalist and anti-semitic deputies who had been returned in 1898; they would be sufficient to give him a majority.

An appeal to nationalist feelings was in any case far from being alien to the bulk of the Radicals; they had inherited the Jacobin tradition of vociferous patriotism confirmed in 1870. Continuing their campaign, commenced during the Panama Affair, of attacking the corruption of the government, they had led the Chamber in its attempt to force Méline to take a stand against the Dreyfusards. In later years the original Dreyfusards were very bitter about the political capital made out of their victory by those who had been their opponents at the time when they needed help. In 1904 Charles Rist wrote to Joseph Reinach, protesting;

> C'est ce même parti radical avec ses Pelletan et ses Goblet qui était à la Chambre la porte-parole des patriotes contre la faiblesse de Méline. C'est lui qui hurlait contre les intellectuels. Aujourd'hui, c'est pour sauver l'influence de ces gens-là et leurs éternels procédés de démagogie que la Ligue se compromet.[10]

Cavaignac, who in 1893 had been one who demanded the most

---

[9] G. Lachapelle, *Le ministère Méline* (1928), p. 175. The posters of the 1898 elections, except for those of Pontevès de Sabran, a Royalist candidate in a poor area, hardly mention Dreyfus.

[10] Bibliothèque Nationale, Reinach Papers, NAF 24882. The "Ligue" referred to was the Ligue des Droits de l'Homme.

drastic measures to clean up corruption, was the incarnation of this Radical nationalism. When he became Minister of War the Brisson ministry was committed to firm opposition to the Dreyfusards. But Cavaignac's assertion that he had definite proofs of Dreyfus' guilt was to make revision inevitable. For it soon emerged that the evidence on which he relied was forged. Henry, the officer responsible for the forgery, committed suicide, Cavaignac resigned, and the government began timidly to set in motion the legal processes which would allow revision.

It was at this time that the campaign against Dreyfus and his defenders became a campaign against the Chamber, the Parliamentary system and perhaps against the Republic itself. In September Déroulède refounded the Ligue des Patriotes which had become inactive after the failure of Boulangism. The Ligue Antisémitique, founded by Jules Guérin in 1897, and used by the count Pontevès de Sabran for his campaign as a royalist in the working class 18th arrondissement in the elections of 1898, suddenly became rich enough to establish its headquarters in the rue Chabrol. Other organisations which were eventually tried for conspiracy were the Ligue de la Défense Nationale founded by a colonel Monteil for his electoral campaign in the 6th arrondissement, the Jeunesses Royalistes which won a certain following of wealthy young men when it broke with the more cautious policy of the older advisers of the Pretender, some Bonapartist committees (but most of their followers had joined the Ligue des Patriotes), and several Socialist groups, listed as the Parti Rochefortiste, the Comité Central Révolutionnaire (part of the old Blanquist committee), the Jeunesse Blanquiste and the Parti Républicain Socialiste Française; finally there was another anti-semitic group, the Jeunesse Antisémite which was mainly a provincial organisation.[11]

All these leagues were mainly devoted to demonstrations in the streets, to holding public meetings and to breaking up meetings of Dreyfusards. The first of their great days was on October 25, 1898, when Parliament reassembled, guarded by a large body of police and troops from the hostile crowds. The Brisson government was replaced by a colourless Republican ministry headed by Dupuy who was determined to avoid trouble. The leagues continued their campaign without any interference, and were joined by a new group the Ligue de la Patrie Française. This new organization was formed for the

[11] Report of the evidence and proceedings of the trial before the High Court of the Senate, published as *Affaire Buffet, Déroulède, Habert et autres* (n.d.).

specific purpose of putting pressure on the government to move the application for reconsideration of Dreyfus' condemnation from the court of criminal appeal to a new court made up of the judges of all three appeal courts, where Quesnay de Beaurepaire had assured them there would be a majority against Dreyfus. It had a more respectable air than the other nationalist leagues in that its leaders were all intellectuals; in many ways they wished to challenge the claim of the Ligue des Droits de l'Homme to represent the intelligence of France. The founders of the Patrie Française were Syveton, Dausset and Vaugeois, all three teachers in Paris lycées; they persuaded Jules Lemaître, a literary critic and François Coppée, a fashionable poet, to become the figureheads of the organisation. Coppée (who was a Catholic and a Bonapartist) was soon pushed into the background as *Président d'honneur*, while Lemaître became the President and effective chief.

While the Ligue de la Patrie Française was elaborating philosophical arguments against those of the Ligue des Droits de l'Homme, the other leagues were forming a plot that involved the Pretender, several army officers and perhaps even the President of the Republic. At least they expected his benevolent neutrality in any enterprise they undertook. The sudden death of Félix Faure in February 1899 put an end to these plans but Déroulède attempted to lead the troops that had been paraded for the funeral in a march on the Elysée that he saw as the signal for a coup d'état.

The last demonstration of the leagues came in June when the new President of the Republic was attacked at the Auteuil race meeting. This incident was to be the turning point in the Affair. It led to the rallying of the Socialists to the Republic. At the Longchamps race meeting the next week the Socialists turned out in thousands to cheer Loubet, not, they pointed out, for himself, but as the symbol of Republican legality. This time the police who had been missing when they were needed to protect the President from the nationalists, were out in force and perhaps from long habit were ready for a battle with the Socialists. The result was a mêlée which led to an interpellation in the Chamber and the fall of the Dupuy government.

Waldeck-Rousseau formed a ministry that was to liquidate the Affair and to put the Republic out of danger. But to find a majority he had to include the Socialist Millerand in the cabinet, thus losing the support of many of the Progressistes. He removed the nationalist leagues from the political scene by arresting their leaders for the conspiracies which he claimed lay behind the demonstrations of February and June. Only the Ligue de la Patrie Française which had not been compromised by this direct action remained in the field.

Thus it became the centre of opposition to the government which had been responsible for the victory of the Dreyfusards. It soon became clear that this meant turning the League into a political party that could compete with the other parties that were formed about this time. Louis Dimier recounts how Vaugeois broke away from the Patrie Française because he refused to admit that they should confine themselves to legal action against the party of Dreyfus.[12] It was on this ground that the Ligue de l'Action Française was founded; it was only some time later that Maurras converted the members to his monarchical theories. But although Dimier says that most of the meeting (convoked by the Patrie Française) applauded Vaugeois' declaration that "il se moquait de l'illégalité", the Action Française was able to win very little attention for several years; it spread by personal contacts among the small circles of intellectuals in which its first members moved.

Until the elections of 1902 the front of the stage was occupied by the Patrie Française. The dominant note of their propaganda was simply opposition to the government that had freed Dreyfus, but the main lines of their policy can be discerned on five sets of questions, though it must be remembered that as Andriveau, their candidate in the 14th arrondissement of Paris, told his electors: "The programme of the Patrie Française is very general; it is a minimum, and each of us has complete liberty to add to it according to his own inclinations." [13] There was no discussion of policy because the membership was never represented in a congress until after the 1902 elections, and even the full committee ceased to meet after the first few weeks.[14]

The most elaborate part of their programme was a plan for reform of the constitution that would prevent the tyranny of either President or Parliament. This result was to be achieved by a separation of powers which would destroy the power of the Assembly to do harm without creating an all-powerful President. The President was not to be elected by the Chambers, but not by a direct vote of the people either. It was to be either the work of special electoral colleges on the American model, or else of a body consisting of the Chamber, the Senate, and other specified groups – usually delegates of the conseils généraux. In addition deputies were to have no right to initiate expenditure, ministers

[12] L. Dimier, Vingt ans d'Action Française et autres souvenirs (1926), pp. 7, 11.

[13] Réveil du 14e., April 27, 1902.

[14] L. Fatoux, Les Coulisses du nationalisme (1903), p. 16.

were to be chosen from outside the Chambers, and to be responsible only to the President. These proposals were an unhappy compromise between those who, like the Ligue des Patriotes, wished to overthrow the whole Parliamentary system, and the conservatives who had no desire for the adventures of a plebiscitary regime. When in 1903, Lemaître made a speech advocating a plebiscitary regime he contributed largely to the collapse of the Patrie Française; many local committees went over to Action Libérale Populaire, the Catholic party, and the resulting divisions allowed the election of a Radical in the Batignolles quartier.[15]

Paradoxically they claimed that they were fundamentally opposed to the existing regime, but at the same time against radical change. In the 14th arrondissement where there were two candidates of the Patrie Française as well as a former Boulangist, there is an exchange that is enlightening on this point. Both candidates accuse the other of wishing to reintroduce "pouvoir personnel"; both hotly deny the charge; at the same time they claim to be fundamentally "anti-Parlementaire".

Of the social and economic policy advocated by the Patrie Française, the two main themes were opposition to collectivism and the danger to small shopkeepers and small businesses represented by the secret alliance of Socialism and Jewish high finance. The echoes roused by this campaign and its evident success among the lower middle class of Paris reveal their anxiety about the future, due more to the development of working class organization and ideology than to purely economic developments. The decisive events were the founding of the Confédération générale du travail, the spread of trade unions, the steps towards the unification of the socialist parties and the presence of Millerand, the man who had laid down the programme of collectivism in a famous speech at St. Mandé, in the government.

The years after 1896 saw a rapid increase in the length, the number, and the bitterness of strikes, and also a rapid expansion of the Socialist group in the Chamber of Deputies. Particularly in Paris was there an increase in the number of strikes. From 1890 to 1895 the number of strikes per 1,000 workers in the Seine department was 8·31, against 24·79 in France as a whole. In 1898, mainly because of a strike of labourers working on railway construction which developed into an attempted general strike, Paris had 62·42 strikers per 1,000 workers against 16·07 in France as a whole. The number of strikers in the Seine

[15] Fatoux, *op. cit.*, pp. 42-3, and *Réveil de Batignolles*, January–July 1903 (passim).

department was 47,189 in 1898, and 27,359 in 1900. In contrast the average for the other nine years of the period 1890–1900, excluding these peak years was only 6,263. The troops were called out and violence developed as a result of which sixty strikers were prosecuted.[16] In 1900 the high figure was not due to any one strike or any particular trade, but to a large number of strikers and of small strikes in different trades, many of which were organized in very small factories, employing skilled craftsmen. One owner of a small workshop complained to the authorities that his twenty workers demonstrated by marching out at the end of each day's work singing the International and behaving with such disrespect that his wife had a nervous collapse and had to retire to her family in the country.[17]

Millerand, at the Bureau du Travail newly erected into a Ministry, embarked on a scheme of social reform which included old age pensions, a limitation of the hours of work, and even a scheme for enforcing a ballot of all the employees of a factory before a strike, the strike then to be unanimous. None of these proposals were passed before 1902, or even seriously discussed by the Assembly, but they were bitterly attacked, together with the income tax, as tyrannous collectivism.

Although this meant that the government lost support on the Right, it also prevented the Nationalists from winning the discontented of both Right and Left as Boulanger had done. The Nationalists attempted this feat; Boulangism was constantly on the lips of their opponents, and no doubt it was in their minds even if they did not care to refer to it. Lemaître's general poster for the 1900 elections contains an appeal to the vote of the Left:

> They call themselves Socialists, and in twenty years they have not achieved a more equal sharing of the burden of taxation, or old age pensions. The Nationalists will embark on these social questions. For Nationalism means care for the interests of all the members of the community. Patriotism involves a spirit of solidarity, mutual aid, and fraternal charity. We advocate a national fund for sickness and unemployment insurance, pensions organized by voluntary societies (*mutualités*): our policy is in everything based on the principle of free association instead of the tyranny of forced Collectivism.[18]

[16] *Statistiques des Grèves* (1898), pp. 156–7, published annually by the Office du Travail, and *Année politique* (1898), p. 325.
[17] *Statistiques des Grèves* (1900), p. 443.
[18] Bibliothèque Historique de la Ville de Paris. Salle 3, Travée D 82.

This poster recapitulates the main themes of the Nationalist campaign with regard to the social question. The actual proposals varied from one candidate to another. One or two denounced the proposed legislation root and branch. Flourens suggested that the plan for old age pensions was a fraud; for the pensions would only be paid at an age so advanced that few would reach it, while the contributions would go to fill the hungry mouths of the *budgétivores*. A common theme was that the able-bodied workman must not be prevented from working as many hours as he wished. So "liberté de travail" was added to the list of "liberté d'enseignement, d'association et de conscience".

But most candidates did not oppose old age pensions, or social legislation, in principle. Instead they emphasized the need for "practical Socialism" against utopian collectivism, for the need to achieve "amélioration sociale", not through class warfare but by the harmonious cooperation of the worker and employer, by giving the worker a share in the benefits of the capital. They also had two specific proposals; the worker, like the capitalist, was to be protected from foreign competition by a tax on the employers of foreign labour; the other was that with the ousting of the corrupt deputies who had destroyed the national wealth by their criminal waste, there would come a golden age of reduced taxation and prosperity for all.

Policy towards the Church was a subject about which the Patrie Française was as deeply divided as it was on the constitutional question. Lemaître himself was a freethinker who had talked of the religion of the *patrie* replacing that of the Church, but Coppée was a Catholic; for that reason he took no active part in the League and was pushed into the background. Among the group of deputies who joined the Nationalists were a majority elected as candidates of the Left in poor areas; the charge of clericalism would be fatal to their prospects of re-election. Yet the bulk of the anti-Dreyfusards who had joined the League were Catholic. Again a policy of compromise was adopted; they insisted that they were anti-clerical. But, they argued, the real danger of clericalism came from the Jews and freemasons, from the sectaries of the Republic, not from the Catholic church. Lemaître advocated the separation of Church and State, provided that it was carried out in a tolerant and generous spirit, as did, of course, most Catholics; to the anticlericals it seemed that what they meant by a tolerant and generous spirit was that the State should continue to pay the salaries of the clergy while renouncing all measures of control over them.

Antisemitism played almost no part in the official policy of the Patrie

Française although they agreed on joint candidatures with several antisemites, and "à bas les juifs" seems to have been a common slogan shouted at their meetings. But in spite of attacks on Jewish high finance they opposed any measures of exception directed against the Jews, and concentrated rather on the danger of foreigners within France.

Finally one comes to the army and foreign affairs which one might expect to find as the central theme of a movement for national revival. Surprisingly, the declared policy of government supporters and of the Nationalists on these questions was almost identical. Both sides insist that they respect the army and wish to see it put outside political quarrels, and both sides demand the reduction of military service. Some Nationalists were prepared to outbid the Radicals and Socialists who were demanding two years' service for all, by calling for fifteen months' or one year's service; some – but not all – of the Nationalists insisted that conscription could only be reduced if sufficient cadres of regular troops had been built up. But the quarrel over the army was mainly concerned with its role in domestic politics. The Nationalists advocated military service as a way of restoring the social discipline which they felt was so lacking in the nation. For the same reasons the Left feared the army as a tool of reaction, while never doubting that it was necessary for national defence. The common feature of all these discussions was that they centred on the political significance of the army rather than on its military efficiency.

This concentration of home affairs was possible because the anti-Dreyfusard Nationalism arose at a time when France's foreign policy was not a crucial question. Rivalry with England had been liquidated at Fashoda. Although this humiliation was an important part of the Nationalist attack on the decadent republic (Fashoda, Panama, Dreyfus, were the three key words in the campaign) they did not in fact advocate a resumption of colonial expansion against England. Any reverse met by England in South Africa was welcomed, and the Boer generals were greeted with great enthusiasm when they visited Paris, but imperial expansion played little part in the Nationalist campaign.[19] Nor did *Revanche*. Alsace-Lorraine had still been an issue in the elections of 1898, when it had been used by the extreme Left against Holtz, the moderate Radical, who won in the 18th arrondissement.[20] In 1902 it hardly seems to have been mentioned, except by one or two candidates

[19] Only two candidates mention colonial expansion in their posters. One, Bonvalot, was himself an African explorer.

[20] Archives Nationales. Enquiry into Holtz's election. C 5361.

who explained their Nationalism by saying that they came from Lorraine. England was the enemy quite as much as Germany, and this remained true for some time after 1905, for newspapers like *la Patrie* and for the propagandists of Action Française.

The Nationalist campaign, although insisting that France should be "strong at home and respected abroad", did not demand that France play a more aggressive role in foreign politics. The tone of the campaign was much more an anxious insistence on the need for national defence. Their opponents recognized that in this they were the true interpreters of public opinion by their counter-attack, which insisted that the Nationalists would embark on military adventure. "A vote for X is a vote for war" was a slogan that was frequently used. Thiébaud, Nationalist candidate in the fifteenth arrondissement, strikes a typical note when he describes Nationalism as "the protest of a nation that does not like to be pushed out of the first rank, that does not wish to die".[21] Flourens, former foreign minister and a successful candidate in the 5th arrondissement, promised that when France returned to her old traditions "she would no longer be condemned to a humiliated silence".[22] And Lemaître wrote in the *Echo de Paris*:

> Nationalism does not mean war. We have too much to do with enemies at home. Our dream is that France become strong, prosperous, united and ordered at home, so that she be respected abroad.[23]

The Nationalists, like the literary polemicists of Action Française,[24] were concerned far more with domestic affairs than with foreign policy, and their attitude towards foreign powers was based on fears of national decadence that would encourage a pacific policy.

III

The municipal elections of 1900 provided the first opportunity for a demonstration of the strength of the rival parties, the Dreyfusards supporting the government and the Nationalists united in opposition. The struggle was fiercest in Paris, for in the provinces passions had never been as much aroused by the Affair as they had in Paris. Besides, the

[21] *Avenir du 15me.*, April 26, 1902.
[22] Bibliothèque Historique de la Ville de Paris, Salle 3, Travée D 83.
[23] *Echo de Paris*, May 8, 1900.
[24] C. Digeon, *La Crise allemande de la pensée française* (1959), p. 448.

municipal council of Paris had expressed its solidarity with the extremists who had extended the fight for Dreyfus into an attack on the army as a whole. In December 1898 the council had decided to buy ninety copies of Urbain Gohier's book, *l'Armée contre la Nation* for the municipal libraries. The motion was carried by 42 votes to 22 with 14 abstentions. Those who opposed the buying of the book were made up of 18 of the 28 members of the Right, with the addition of three Radicals and one Socialist; the remaining Socialists voted for the book, as did the majority of the Radicals, though the bulk of the abstainers were Radicals. This vote was a major part of the Nationalist campaign, and one of their most widely distributed posters consisted of extracts from Gohier's book together with a list of councillors who had voted for its purchase. The two Radicals who had voted against the book were spared a Nationalist opponent in the 1900 elections, although they later rejoined the *bloc*.

The elections proved to be the victory for which the Nationalists had hoped. All but three of the retiring councillors stood for re-election, but thirty seats out of the eighty changed hands – about three times the normal proportion. There was much surprise at the result, which was commented on at length by all the newspapers. The Nationalists insisted on the role of Paris as the leader of opinion, and claimed a moral defeat for the government, while the republican papers pointed out that Paris had already supported Boulanger and not been followed by steadier rural voters. The comment of *le Temps* was that

la capitale avait voté dans un de ses jours de fronde et de boutade.[25]

The central groups, Radicals and Républicains Municipaux were the chief victims of the Nationalists. The Républicains Municipaux disappeared altogether – naturally enough as their chief slogan was that politics had no place at the Hôtel de Ville. The three councillors who did not stand for re-election belonged to this group, and were succeeded by Nationalists. Five of them campaigned as anti-Dreyfusards and joined the Nationalist group in the new council, and the remaining six were easily defeated. The Radicals, who had been thirty-three in 1896, were reduced to twenty-three before the elections, through by-elections and the defection of six of their members to the Socialist group. The election reduced them to sixteen. The Socialists retained twenty of their twenty-six councillors – they had four gains, balanced by ten losses, six at the polls and four who were re-elected but joined the

[25] *Le Temps*, May 8, 1900.

Radical group. The frontiers between Radicalism and Socialism were of the vaguest, and as J. E. C. Bodley pointed out, the most expert observer could hardly distinguish them.[26]

Out of the thirty newly elected councillors twenty-five were Nationalist, one was a Bonapartist, and four were Socialist. The Nationalist group numbered thirty-six, made up of their twenty-five new men, one who had been elected for the first time as a Nationalist in 1899, five who had been Républicains Municipaux, four who had been conservative, and one who had been Socialist. This latter, Gré-bauval, the living proof that the Nationalists were not reactionary, was elected the President of the council by the new majority.

A comparison of the quartiers won by the Nationalists with the social classification of the quartiers reveals the predominantly middle class character of their support. The wealthiest areas did not vote for Nationalists for they were already in most cases represented by conservatives who were firmly anti-Dreyfusard. On the other hand, only six of the Nationalists were elected by quartiers classed by Bertillon as poor, while the councillors elected in poor areas in 1896 who went over to Nationalism were defeated with the exception of Grébauval. But fifteen out of twenty-two prosperous quartiers, and six out of eight rich ones were represented by Nationalists. Only eight out of fifteen quartiers classed by Bertillon as very rich had Nationalist councillors, but their other councillors were anti-Dreyfusard conservatives.

An analysis of the movement of votes over the whole of Paris reveals that the Nationalist success was based largely on existing conservative and radical tendencies. The votes are given in the following table, with percentages calculated on the number of people voting:

	1896	1900	1904
Nationalist	—	34·21	32·89
Conservative	33·09	7·2	11·47
Radical	29·42	20·21	17·7
Socialist	35·58	30·53	34·0

N.B. Only serious candidates are counted, i.e. those with about 200 votes in the quartiers with the smallest population, rather more in the more populous ones. The fall in the sum of the percentage for 1900 reveals the large number of 'mushroom' candidates brought out by the excited political atmosphere; the temperature was lower in 1904, but not back to the calm of 1896.

[26] J. E. C. Bodley, *France* (2nd edition, 1902), p. 622.

The sudden drop in the percentage of conservative votes is due partly to the fact that in 1900 many who had previously campaigned under various conservative labels now stood as Nationalists – this applies to a host of unsuccessful candidates as well as to those who were elected. The small decline in the Socialist share of the vote is partly explained by the fact that there was no serious Nationalist candidate, with a newspaper or an active campaign of public meetings and posters, in nine of the poor quartiers. In the rich areas where there was no Nationalist candidate, this was because the sitting councillor was already firmly anti-Dreyfusard.

When the Nationalist votes are compared, quartier by quartier with the votes cast for the candidate in that quartier most to the Right in 1896, it is confirmed that the Nationalists won the votes that already went to the Right. The difference was that in 1896 this may have been a Radical as against a Socialist, so that once elected he would take up a position on the Left of the municipal council. The Nationalists, in spite of their protests against being classed as reactionaries, joined with the old councillors of the Right to outvote the old alliance of Radicals and Socialists that controlled the council. Thus rather than being the result of a violent change in the loyalties of a fickle city, the Nationalist victory reflected the swing of a fairly small portion of the electorate which was enough to change the balance of power in the council. By providing a new issue on which Republicans could ally with the old Right anti-Dreyfusism became a bridge over which Republican voters were brought to support a new alliance against that of the Radicals and Socialists.

When the conflict in 1896 had been between extreme Right and Left (e.g. between a Socialist and a conservative), the Nationalists considerably extended the vote of the Right. But when the conflict in 1896 had been between a Radical and a Socialist the Nationalist collected some but not all of the Radical vote. A comparison of the votes at the two ballots in 1900 also brings out the fact that a Nationalist standing at the second ballot would usually collect the whole vote cast for conservative candidates at the first ballot.[27] Standing against a Socialist

[27] The electoral system for both municipal and legislative elections was as follows: if no candidate received an absolute majority of the *suffrages exprimés* (i.e. valid votes, excluding spoiled papers) there was a second ballot a week later in the case of municipal elections, a fortnight later for legislative elections. Any number of candidates could stand at the second ballot, without having stood at the first, but a simple majority ensured election. So, in practice, the two strongest

at the second ballot he could hope to get half or more of the votes of a Radical who had stood down, even if the latter had asked his electors to support the Socialist. But there was a certain amount of support for Nationalism from the extreme Left. In opposition to a Radical at the second ballot a Nationalist sometimes collected up to a third of the Socialist votes, especially if they had been cast for a Blanquist who was equally anti-ministerial.

Thus in conclusion it may be said that Nationalism in Paris in the elections of 1900 was in complete contrast to Boulangism. The latter had been supported by the extremes of Right and Left, rejected by the Centre. Nationalism was basically a movement of the Right, and received all the votes that would normally have been cast for a conservative candidate; it extended the domain of the Right, splitting the Radical votes between those who voted right against collectivism, and the attack on national and social order, and those who voted left against the danger of clerical reaction. It also momentarily won some votes from the extreme Left, only to lose them in 1904 because of its association with the Right. The 15th arrondissement, where Boulanger's margin over the conservative vote in 1885 was the highest in Paris, was one of the areas where Nationalism had the least success.[28] Both deputy and councillor, elected as Socialists, turned to Nationalism and were defeated. On the other hand, the commercial areas of central Paris in the 3rd and 10th arrondissements which had given Boulanger the least support became Nationalist strongholds, and even Brisson was turned out of the seat that had been his since 1876, opposed by two nobodies who had both long been contesting the seat without success.

The victory of 1900 encouraged the Patrie Française to embark on a full-scale campaign for the legislative elections of 1902; it became a political party, the most violent and aggressive, if not the most successful, of the opposition parties. Barrès, who did not approve of this electoral activity, which could, he said, only have the result of replacing Waldeck-Rousseau by Ribot and Méline "who are the other side of the same coin", resigned from the committee.[29]

candidates of the rival tendencies at the first ballot, fought it out at the second; if other candidates stood they were, in 1902, ignored by the electors. L. Duguit, M. Monnier, R. Bonnard, *Les constitutions et les principales lois politiques de la France depuis 1789* (7th edition, 1952), p. 304.

[28] L. Giard, *Les Elections à Paris, 1871–1939* (Unpublished thesis), p. 53.

[29] M. Barrès, *Scènes et Doctrines du Nationalisme* (n.d.), p. 95.

Cavaignac, Lemaître, and other leading speakers of the movement visited most parts of France, and hoped to institute candidates in most areas.

According to the results of the election given by *le Temps* there were one hundred and nine Nationalist candidates outside the department of Seine, of whom thirty were elected at the first ballot and nine others at the second. This was not a negligible result for a new party, but it soon became clear that individual candidates outside Paris owed their success more to their personal position than to the patronage of the Patrie Française. *Les coulisses du nationalisme*, a pamphlet written by Léon Fatoux, an officer of the Vincennes garrison who resigned from the army in 1900 in order to devote himself to organizing the Patrie Française, describes the chaos that ruled around Lemaître and Syveton; it was the court of King Pétaud, he says. It is interesting that Fatoux explains that he had been convinced by Doumer's Radical campaign of 1896 (which was directed against the Senate) that the Parliamentary regime was the source of French weakness. He hoped that the Patrie Française would win the support of the working classes, and resigned when the first congress of the League in 1903 revealed the bitter hostility of its members to any measure of social reform, and their enthusiasm for "défense religieuse". He wrote his pamphlet to justify his resignation and in his disappointment judges the Patrie Française very harshly. But he shows quite clearly that the organization was only effective in the department of the Seine, and that outside certain constituencies in the Paris area, the Patrie Française won little support beyond the circles of the Catholic bourgeoisie.

The difference in the Paris area was that there was no rival organization of conservatives. The Progressistes (and their rivals the Alliance démocratique) had no strongholds at all; nor had the Catholics yet any support for Action libérale populaire. Except in the 7th, 8th, 9th and 16th arrondissements the whole Parliamentary representation of Paris was of the Left. The municipal elections had proved the value of the patronage of the Patrie Française in the prosperous areas, and the newspapers *l'Intransigeant* and *Libre Parole* provided a large audience for Nationalist propaganda.

In order to co-ordinate the campaign a committee was formed to discuss candidates. It consisted of Lemaître, Cavaignac, Galli (the leader of the Ligue des Patriotes now that Déroulède was in exile), Drumont of the *Libre Parole*, and Rochefort of the *Intransigeant*, together with the existing nationalist deputies and sympathetic notables.

In the end there was not much co-ordination, as Lemaître was never able to make up his mind. In three constituencies rival candidates were both able to claim the support of the Patrie Française. André Berthelot, elected for the 6th arrondissement as a Radical, but not a member of any group in the Chamber, dragged out negotiations with Lemaître without committing himself. The Patrie Française committee in his constituency was dissolved and no candidate put forward. The result was that Charles Benoist won the seat as a candidate of "national and social defence", although his chances had seemed very slim.[30] Puech, a Radical, had committed himself a good deal further than Berthelot (by introducing an amendment to the law on Associations making all associations legal without authorization, thus destroying the anti-clerical nature of the bill). He was opposed by an official Radical candidate, but nevertheless was forced back into the *bloc* because Dausset, having won his seat in the council in Puech's constituency, wished to stand for the Chamber there.[31]

Fatoux complained that mediocrities, who seeing the success of 1900, sprang up everywhere, were given patronage and financial support, while men (like Fatoux himself) who had worked hard to build up the organization were given the posts of honour in solidly proletarian constituencies. Control of the purse should have enabled the central committee to discipline the local groups, but the treasurer, Syveton, disrupted the organization in order to build a private empire. The head offices of the League which were in the hands of Dausset became a backwater, while Syveton's office for his campaign in the 2nd arrondissement was full of prospective candidates queuing up for subsidies.[32]

Although the Patrie Française claimed to have a committee in each of the eighty quartiers the organisation was really confined to the more prosperous districts. In the poorer areas the Nationalist candidates did not usually claim the support of the Patrie Française, and when they did so it was usually with little success. The usual title of a Nationalist in a poor area was "Socialiste Patriote" or "Socialiste Antiministériel". Most of the Nationalist candidates who won a sizeable vote in poor

[30] On Benoist's campaign his *Souvenirs*, Vol. III (1934), pp. 15-19. The estimate of his prospects by the Prefecture is in Institut MSS 4614 (1). Berthelot's negotiations are revealed by the news-sheet of Alliance Républicaine Démocratique, March 14, 1902.

[31] Fatoux, *op. cit.*, p. 33. Puech's amendment, *Journal Officiel*, January 29, 1901.

[32] Fatoux, *op. cit.*, pp. 34-5.

areas had been active in politics there in earlier elections, as Boulangists, Blanquists, or as Radicals campaigning against the extremes of collectivist socialism. On the other hand in the prosperous areas many candidates were new men who had no previous political career, in that area at least; several (Archdeacon, Flourens, Auffray) had come from the provinces.

The result of the elections of 1902 was similar to that of 1900. The majority among the deputies of Paris went from left to right. Before the elections Paris had twelve deputies inscribed in Socialist groups in the Chamber, and seven in Radical groups; together with Berthelot and Puech elected as Radicals and Millerand who had left the Socialist group on joining the cabinet there were twenty-two deputies of the Left; the Right had fourteen, including six Nationalists who had been elected as candidates of the Left; the other members of the Right were two Progressistes, two members of the Catholic group Action libérale populaire, one Royalist and one Bonapartist, and two Nationalists of the Right (Millevoye and Berry).

After the elections there were ten Socialists, seven Radicals, six Conservatives, two Antiministerials, and fifteen Nationalists, making twenty-three of the Right against seventeen of the Left. As in 1900 the Nationalists represented the more prosperous areas; only four of them had a majority in quarters classed as poor, while four out of the six deputies elected on the Left in 1898 who joined the Nationalists were defeated. Paris was for the first time clearly divided politically on social and economic lines. With the exception of the Bel Air quartier on the edge of the Bois de Vincennes, slightly more prosperous than its neighbours but still sharing their ideals, and of the 3rd arrondissement, where the Radical Puech survived partly because he had opposed the Waldeck-Rousseau government, every prosperous and rich quartier was represented by a Nationalist or a Conservative, while with the exceptions mentioned above, every poor quartier had given a majority to a Radical or a Socialist.

The movement of votes in the whole of Paris is given in the following table:

	1898	1902	1906
Nationalist	3·2	37·16	25·39
Conservative	21·97	12·54	16·04
Radical	25·38	18·69	25·29
Socialist	38·44	27·97	30·46

When these figures are compared with those of the municipal elections of 1900 there is a striking similarity in the total Nationalist vote. The fate of the other parties however, was rather different. The various conservative candidates lost much less than in the municipal elections, but were fewer to start with; in fact no solidly based Conservative candidate lost to a Nationalist; Muzet, who was defeated, had won his seat only in 1898; the Nationalist candidate failed to unseat Beauregard, in spite of the forecast of the prefect; while in the 4th arrondissement the honour of defeating the Radical in possession went to a local businessman, Failliot, and not to either of the official Nationalist candidates.[33] The Radical vote fell in almost the same proportion as in 1900, but the Socialist fell a good deal more than two years earlier, partly because in 1902 there was a Nationalist candidate in every constituency where the sitting deputy had supported the government; in 1900 there had been nine quartiers where there was no anti-Dreyfusard candidate.

A comparison of votes at the first and second ballots again shows that in a run-off between a Nationalist and a candidate of the other extreme the Nationalist would collect half the centre vote. Archdeacon got half of the Progressiste vote against a Radical; Auffray got half the Radical vote against the Socialist Viviani. But when the second ballot was between a Nationalist and a Radical, the Nationalist usually managed to win a certain number of Socialist votes. In the one case where a Nationalist retired at the second ballot to leave a Royalist in the field, his vote split equally, half to the Socialist, and half to the Royalist. When the Nationalist vote is compared with the vote for the candidate most to the right in that area in 1898, it emerges that, as in 1900, they were building on the existing conservative vote.

Only in one area is there an exception to the general rule that the Nationalists were most successful in the prosperous areas. This is the north-eastern district beyond the Gare de l'Est, where is to be found the constituency which Holtz won from the Socialist Lavy in 1898 as a Radical, held in 1902 as a Nationalist, and passed on to his friend Bussat in 1906. It contained four poor quartiers that elected Nationalist councillors in 1900, two of whom survived in 1904, and one (Grébauval) down to 1914. Two other quartiers gave a large minority of their votes to Nationalist candidates in 1900, as did the whole area in 1902, while a little to the west is Epinettes where Roche held his seat

<hr />

[33] The Prefect forecast defeat for both Beauregard and Failliot. Institut, Waldeck-Rousseau Papers, MSS 4614 (1).

as a Nationalist in 1902 – although the councillor for the same constituency was the Socialist Brousse who defeated Roche for the
Parliamentary seat in 1906, only to lose it again to Roche in 1910.
Obviously the personal position of the candidates was more important
than their party labels in this area.

One explanation given for the Nationalist success is that the area
contained a large number of foreigners whose presence was resented.
Guixou-Pagès, who campaigned here as a Royalist, mentions this, and
the fact that Holtz and Bussat made a special point of demanding
legislation to protect the French worker from the foreigner.[34] However
this may be, according to the figures given by L. Chevalier, there was
not an unusually high proportion of foreigners in the area, nor an
especially large number of people born outside Paris.[35] The provincials
who lived here were probably from Alsace, Lorraine, or the eastern
provinces, where Nationalism made a strong appeal. But the posters
preserved show no trace of an appeal to *revanchard* feeling in 1900 and
1902, although in 1898 there had been a special poster appealing for the
vote of people from Alsace and Lorraine – directed against Holtz who
was accused of wishing to appease Germany.[36]

In fact the most important reason for the Nationalist success here was
the nature of the industrial occupations of the area. It was an area of
heavy industry requiring large numbers of unskilled workers – gas
works, slaughter-houses and docks. The butchers were especially ready
to follow the Nationalists and their importance in the antisemitic
gangs had been noticed from 1890 onwards. But the other workers of
the area were largely outside the organised Socialist movement; most
of the members of the Paris Bourse du Travail belonged to skilled
trades, and worked in small workshops.[37] Guixou-Pagès describes how
the dockers and labourers of La Villette were recruited and paid by
foremen contractors who were able to resist all attempts at unionisa-
tion.[38] Thus although this was one of the poorest areas in Paris, and
one which had first sent Socialists to the Hôtel de Ville, it was one where
the personal position of the candidate was all important. Although
Grébauval was elected president of the municipal council by the

[34] Guixou-Pagès, *Chez les gars de la Villette* (1900), pp. 109–13.
[35] L. Chevalier, *Formation de la population parisienne* (1950), p. 287.
[36] Archives Nationales C 5361, evidence produced in protest against Holtz's
election.
[37] L. Le Thouff, *Histoire du Bourse du Travail de Paris* (1902), pp. 96–101.
[38] Guixou-Pagès, *op. cit.*, pp. 114–16.

Nationalists he could still call himself a Socialist in his electoral campaigns in Le Combat.

IV

The years after 1902 saw the rapid collapse of the Nationalist movement as represented by the Patrie Française, although individuals elected under their auspices continued to be successful. About fifty Nationalists were elected to the Chamber, but although they formed a parliamentary group it was of little importance. For the parties of the Left had a sure majority, and the Nationalists were confined to the role of a bitter opposition, together with the other members of the Right. Many members of the Nationalist group belonged to other groups of the Right, and after the 1906 elections several of those who were re-elected failed to join the Nationalist group. In 1910, when deputies had to choose one group for the purpose of electing parliamentary committees, the Nationalist group disappeared.

The absorption of the Nationalists by the other groups of the Right was not surprising. For no one factor distinguished those elected as Nationalists from the other members of the Right. They were not more concerned with national defence. Archdeacon, the Nationalist deputy for Paris, opened the attack on Delcassé in April 1905, later to be regarded as a humiliating capitulation before the demands of Germany.[39] Their constitutional ideas were not deeply held, and all unity on this subject was destroyed when Lemaître, without consulting anyone, announced his conversion to a plebiscitary regime. Their special position with regard to the clerical question was denied when they nearly all voted against separation of Church and State – including some who had demanded it in their election manifestos. While their anti-collectivism and opposition to income tax were common to most of the Right and Centre.

In the Paris municipal council the Nationalists had a majority, and were not confined to opposition. But here they were embarrassed by their desire to prove that they were not of the Right, and by the limitations on the power of the council whose decisions were subject to the approval of the Prefect. The tactics of the Left were designed to prove that their conquerors were clerical reactionaries. At one of the

[39] B. R. Leaman, "The Influence of Domestic Policy in Foreign Affairs in France", in *Journal of Modern History*, Vol. 14 (1942), pp. 449–79.

first meetings of the new Council, Navarre, the leader of the Left, introduced the proposal that

> le conseil émit le voeu que le droit d'enseigner soit retiré aux congrégations non autorisés, que les biens de mainmort fassent retour à la nation.[40]

Four Nationalists voted for this expression of opinion which of course had no practical effect, and three abstained.

The Council was paying subsidies to several organizations such as the Ligue de la Libre Pensée, societies for the encouragement of secular education, Masonic orphanages, training schools for nurses to replace nuns in hospitals and to the Bourse du Travail. The new majority wished to reduce or abolish these subsidies on grounds of economy, and because they disapproved of most of the objects supported. In the end very few of the subsidies were cut off entirely, as a number of the Nationalists were afraid of the charge of clericalism. The subsidy to the Bourse du Travail was however, cut off, and the money paid into a special fund from which subsidies could be paid to individual unions of which the council approved. It seems that there were very few genuine applications, so the fund remained undistributed, while the government took over the subsidy to the Bourse du Travail.

The Nationalists put up a stronger fight over the matter of renewing the contract of the company which provided Paris with gas. Against the bitter opposition of the Left, they voted a scheme which would reduce the price of gas to the consumer by a third. The Left argued that this only showed the immense profits that the company had been making, and that if the council took over the industry the price could be reduced still further. The government vetoed the project voted by the council, so that Nationalists in 1902 were able to include opposition to a reduction of the price of gas among the misdeeds of the Waldeck-Rousseau government. But in 1903 the council adopted the proposal of the Left for a municipal gas supply, with eight Nationalists voting for it, and three abstaining.

At the elections of 1904 the Nationalists lost control of the Council although the votes cast changed very little (see table, p. 68). In all twelve seats changed hands of which nine were Nationalist losses, four to Radicals, three to Socialists, and two to Conservatives. The new council was made up of twenty-six Socialists, eighteen Radicals, twenty-three Nationalists and thirteen Conservatives. The changes

[40] *Bulletin Municipal Officiel* (1900), p. 2079.

emphasize the middle class nature of Nationalist support; there were now only three Nationalist councillors for poor quartiers.

The legislative elections of 1906 confirmed that the nationalism of the Patrie Française was a spent force. The organization had collapsed on the death of Syveton in 1905, and Lemaître was moving steadily towards royalism. The young and active who had joined the League in the exciting days of the Affair were now attracted either to Action Française or to various Catholic groups. There was no common Nationalist organization for the 1906 election, only the individual campaigns of those who had been elected in 1902 and some hopeful candidates who had missed the tide then; the latter were universally unsuccessful. Nevertheless, individual Nationalist candidates in prosperous and rich areas, retained and even extended their votes. The Radicals recovered many more votes than the Socialists (see table, p. 73) and five Radicals held seats which had been Socialist in 1898.

In 1906 as in 1904, Nationalists no longer attracted Radical and Socialist votes at the second ballot. Many of the old Radical voters had gone over to the Nationalists in 1902. Those who remained loyal to the Left at the first ballot cast their votes for the Left at the second; their choice had been made, while the Nationalists were now completely identified with the Right, and were unable to win any votes from the extreme Left. There were fifteen quartiers where the Nationalist percentage of votes increased in 1906: eight were rich, six prosperous and one poor. The latter was Chapelle – the constituency which Holtz handed on to his friend Bussat. Bussat joined no group in the Chamber, but was usually associated with the Radicals, and his seat on the Municipal council was won by a Socialist; it was entirely his personal position that accounted for the Nationalist success in this area. In nearly all the other poor quartiers the Nationalist vote fell heavily. Nine of the fifteen Nationalists were re-elected, but only five joined the Nationalist group in the Chamber.

While on the municipal council the Nationalists were steadily absorbed by the other conservative groups. Nine of the Nationalists joined the group of Républicains Anti-collectivistes formed by some of those who had been Républicains Municipaux before 1900. The Left remained in control of the council from 1904 to 1909, and the President was alternately a Radical and a Socialist. A trivial incident was the occasion for the Right to gain control of the council, which it never afterwards lost. In 1909 the President was the Socialist Chausse; he tried to associate the council in a gesture of sympathy with Francisco

Ferrer, the Spanish anarchist executed for moral support of the Barcelona rising, by naming a Paris street after him. He was defeated when five Radicals voted against him, and four others abstained. Chausse resigned, and E. Caron who had been a Républicain Municipal and then a Nationalist was elected President. The manifesto issued by the dissident Radicals shows the general considerations about the co-operation of the Radical party with the Socialists which had influenced their stand on this symbolic matter; they declared

> that as Radical republicans elected with a clearly anti-collectivist mandate, we cannot, without betraying it, ally with those whose demands grow day by day and whose aim is the overturning of present society without any indication of what the future society will be.[41]

Thus it was not strictly the Nationalism of the Dreyfus Affair that swung the municipal council of Paris from Left to Right, but a further split in the Paris Radicals over the question of the alliance with the Socialists, when there was no longer a danger that joining the Right meant joining a coalition that included those who threatened the existence of the Republic.[42] The security of the Right's hold over the council from this time onwards was partly due to the fact that each quartier had one councillor whatever its population. As the population of the poor districts of the outer quartiers increased, they became less and less fairly represented as against the prosperous and rich quartiers where the population grew much more slowly, or in some cases even decreased.

V

The correlation between voting habits and social class is not an easy one to make, especially for a time when there is no more precise information than that which refers to the voting and economic status of a whole quartier of a city. Modern enquiries have shown that even where the lines of class are most strongly drawn, identification of a whole social group with one political tendency is very rare – in France, at least. Nevertheless with these provisos, it can be established that the

[41] *Le Petit Temps*, November 4, 1909.
[42] Standard accounts often ignore the victory of the Left in 1904; cf. R. Rémond, *La Droite en France de 1815 à nos jours* (1954), p. 156.

Nationalist movement in Paris in these years appealed particularly to the middle and lower middle classes of the city. The very rich areas of the 7th and 8th arrondissements, the home of the wealthy upper bourgeoisie, had always voted for conservative candidates and been hostile to the Republic. The poorest areas, with the exceptions mentioned above where Nationalism appeared to be a movement of the Left, did not vote for Nationalists in 1900 and 1902, although they had supported Boulanger. It was in the areas of moderate income, where the average family had one or two domestic servants, where there were large numbers of small shopkeepers and businessmen and white-collar workers, that the success of the Nationalists was most striking. But wherever the sitting candidate in the wealthy areas could be identified with support for the Dreyfusards the success of the Nationalist opponent was even more complete.

A more detailed analysis of the voting swings reveals that what happened was that the radical vote split. Brisson's constituency provides a good example:

1898			*1902*		
Brisson (Radical) . . .	6917		Brisson (Radical) . . .	5362
Roldes (Socialist) . . .	1833		Tournade (Nationalist) .	4258
Houdé (Rep.)	1669		Houdé (Nationalist) . .	3443
Briançon (Rallié.) . . .	859		Vannier (Guesdiste) . .	283

N.B. Votes are for the first ballot; in 1902 the Nationalist vote united to elect Tournade at the second ballot.

In 1898 Brisson was the Centre candidate elected with a sure majority over the two extremes as he had been for twenty years; in 1902 he is the candidate of the Left and is defeated. His defeat was typical; in general all those who had previously voted for conservative Republican candidates supported the Nationalists; in addition about a third or a half of the Radical vote went to the Nationalists.

This movement to the Right had commenced in 1898. Then it had been at the expense of the Socialists and in favour of the Radicals in the poorer areas, and at the expense of the Radicals in favour of conservative republicans in the richer areas. In 1902 the Radicals were hopelessly compromised by their association with the Socialists in the cabinet, and in the *bloc des gauches*; so the anti-collectivist vote went to the Nationalists. But the Radicals had a weapon with which to fight back; it was anticlericalism. In 1902 the Nationalists denied that they were clericals and most of them advocated the separation of Church and State in some form. By 1906 they were definitely associated with the clerical camp; on the other hand the cry of collectivism was no longer so dangerous to the Radicals. The Socialists were no longer represented in the Cabinet, Millerand had ceased to be a dangerous revolutionary, and four years of government by the Left had seen the foundations of society untouched – old age pensions and income tax were still a long way in the future. So the Radicals were able to re-cover some of their seats in the border areas, especially where there was a large working-class element in the constituency that would vote Radical at the second ballot. But apart from a few fluctuations in these mixed constituencies the political frontiers remained in their main lines as they had been defined in 1902. The majority of the voters won to the Right remained loyal, but there were few new gains.

Other evidence of the Nationalist appeal to the middle classes comes from their propaganda. They emphasize the difficulties of the tax-payer and the ratepayer, and demand a strong government that will put an end to waste in the administration and reduce taxes. The difficulties that were facing "petit commerce" were a common theme, and they were overjoyed when *l'Aurore* made the mistake of attacking shopkeepers for their treachery after the first ballot of the 1902 elections; the more insulting phrases of the article were posted on the walls of every constituency where there was to be a second ballot, with a list of the candidates supported by *l'Aurore* so that the shopkeepers could vote accordingly. Several candidates protested that they could not help being supported by *l'Aurore* and that they were very far from sharing its views about "petit commerce". In spite of the Nationalist appeal to "petit commerce" though, the most powerful organization of small shopkeepers, the Comité de l'Alimentation only supported one or two Nationalist candidates. Only the association of Commerçants Etala-gistes were unanimously for the Nationalists as their members had been annoyed by some new regulations about stallholding.

Why then was the Nationalist movement of the Patrie Française so much more successful in Paris than in the provinces, and why did its success prove to be so ephemeral? The answer to the first question is that in Paris before 1900 the forces of the Right hardly existed outside the wealthiest areas, except in the form of Radicals and moderate Republicans who were compromised by association with the govern-ment of Waldeck-Rousseau. Nationalists stood as representatives of the forces of "order" in spite of being against the government. For their charge was that the government had fallen into the hands of those who were conniving at the dissolution of society. They appealed not to those who wished to embark on dangerous political adventures, but to those who wished to resist a dangerous socialist government. Thus, in spite of the charges of their opponents, they were not aiming at the overthrow of the Republic, although their proposals for constitutional reform were compromised by their association with others who were anti-Republican.[43]

Nationalism succeeded in different regions of France for different reasons. Towards the eastern frontier it was the direct result of the anti-militarism of the Dreyfusards. In the towns of the West, Siegfried found that Nationalism repeated the success of Boulangism in swinging normally Republican seats to the Right by adding urban demagogy to a rural conservative vote in mixed town and country constituencies.[44]

In Paris the movement of the Patrie Française was accorded the title of Nationalist only because of the special circumstances of the Dreyfus Affair. There was very little in their programme which appealed specifically to nationalist feelings, and the whole tone of their campaign was very different from the *revanchard* atmosphere that had followed 1870. Benoist, who appealed to the same voters as the Patrie Française called himself the candidate of "national and social defence", and this combination best sums up the Nationalist campaign. The need for strong government, and for a more authoritarian social system, and above all the need to resist collectivism were the elements in their programme that appealed to the conservative voters of Paris.

The same analysis reveals the reason for the fading away of Nationalism as a movement; their representatives were indistinguishable from the other deputies and councillors of the Right. Those Nationalists who had originally been men of the Left were either defeated at the polls or became absorbed by the Right, in the same way as did Rochefort, who from being in 1880 the journalist of the intransigent Left, ended by writing for the bourgeois newspaper, *la Patrie*.[45]

Nationalism was something that divided the electorate more than it united them. For the Revolution had left behind a nationalist tradition as strong as that of the *ancien régime*, and the Patrie Française in 1900 could be denounced as the heir of the *chouans* and *émigrés* who had

[43] Léon Blum, "Les élections de 1902" in *L'Œuvre de Léon Blum*, Vol. 1 (1954), p. 498: "La coalition conservatrice est unie solidement par un programme, mais dans ce programme le renversement de la République ne figure point."
[44] A. Siegfried, *Tableau Politique de la France de l'Ouest* (1913), pp. 491–3.
[45] A. Zévaés, *Henri Rochefort, le pamphlétaire* (1946), pp. 246–7.

fought against France at the time of her greatest glory. Barrès denounced the intellectuals who formed in their own brains a conception of France into which they then tried to mould their fellow-citizens. But the Nationalist project was nothing more than a rival intellectual conception. Radicals, and even Socialists were very far from rejecting the necessity of national defence and of prestige and expansion.

It has been pointed out that nationalism in France has been associated more with opposition than with either the Left or the Right as such.[46] Both 1830 and 1848 saw oppositions that had invoked nationalist feelings abandon their policies when suddenly brought to power. For the great difficulty of French governments in the nineteenth century was that ever since the days of Napoleon memories of national grandeur had been out of proportion with the power and resources of the country. Rulers had to choose between following a cautious policy, thus leaving themselves open to nationalist *surenchère*, and risking everything in an adventurous foreign policy, as did Napoleon III. But when, as in 1870, or again during the first World War, there was a real and immediate danger, the whole nation united in self-defence. It was in times when the danger was not so urgent that there was room for conflicts of opinion, in which both sides adopted extreme positions. The argument over nationalism provoked by the Dreyfus Affair came at just such a time when feeling about Alsace-Lorraine and desire to avenge the defeat of 1870 had almost died away, and before the series of crises that preceded the first World War had begun.

Comparison of the political geography of Paris after the Nationalist victories of 1900 and 1902 with the earlier explosion of nationalism in the election of Boulanger on January 27, 1889 shows that the last decade of the nineteenth century had worked a complete transformation of the political scene. Boulanger had been supported by the Right (almost unanimously, while in the general elections of the autumn individual Boulangist condidates were not all so successful), by nearly all the Socialists and by about half the Radicals.[47] In the whole belt of poor areas around the perimeter of the city he had a substantial margin over the vote of the conservative candidate in 1885. This margin was greatest in the new and rapidly developing industrial suburbs in the 15th arrondissement. The areas in which Boulanger was least successful

[46] R. Girardet, "Pour une introduction à l'histoire du nationalisme français" in *Revue Française de Science Politique*, Vol. VIII (1958), pp. 505–28.

[47] A. Dansette, *Le Boulangisme* (1946), p. 253 n. 2; and map in the thesis of L. Giard, *Les Elections à Paris, 1871–1939*.

were the 3rd and the 10th arrondissements, the centres of small and medium commerce, of small workshops and independant artisans. It was exactly in these areas that the anti-Dreyfusard nationalists were most successful; although Puech, the Radical deputy of the 3rd arrondissement retained his seat by skilful equivocation, the surrounding areas were all won by Nationalists, even against Radicals like Brisson and Mesureur who had long been undisputed masters of their constituencies. While in the 15th arrondissement, although both deputy and councillor who had been elected on the Left became Nationalist, no Nationalist was successful in 1900 and 1902.

It was the development of Socialist organization that prevented the Nationalists from winning the working class support that had gone to Boulanger. It was no longer possible to assemble a union of the discontented including both extreme Right and Left. Hostility to the Dreyfusards had at first been strong on the Left; out of the six Paris deputies elected in 1898 who joined the nationalist group in the Chamber, four had been elected as Radicals or Socialists. But as the Nationalist campaign turned into an attack on the institutions of the Republic the Radicals abandoned their demands for constitutional revision, and the Socialists began to moderate their criticism of the existing regime. In the words of Waldeck-Rousseau, with the formation of his government they began to take over the Republic, to make it their own.[48]

Thus the result of the Nationalist campaign was to divide Paris politically along the same lines as those that separated areas of different economic and social conditions. From Batignolles in the north around the eastern and southern perimeter of the city, and touching the working class suburbs beyond the city boundary, there was the 'red belt' that voted to the Left; in the central areas, and towards the west, there were the middle class constituencies that voted for Nationalists or conservatives. The few working class areas that voted Nationalist in 1900 and 1902 were virtually won over to the left by 1906. This division was in the end fatal to the Radicals who had depended on the votes of both middle class and working class. They were gradually pushed out of Paris to become the party of the small provincial town. But this was a slow process, and was by no means completed in 1914.

[48] Letter to J. Reinach, quoted by him in his *Histoire de l'Affaire Dreyfus*, Vol. V, p. 171, note 2.

© D. R. WATSON 1962

THE RIGHT AND THE SOCIAL QUESTION IN PARLIAMENT, 1905-1919

by Malcolm Anderson

I

THE SEPARATION of the Churches and the State became law in December 1905. In that month the liberal monarchist, Denys Cochin, wrote to the daughter of Albert de Mun:

> Vous sortez de la Chambre épouvanté de ce qui s'est dit et se prépare. Vous rencontrez des gens qui battissent, labourent, boursicotent, comme si de rien n'était. Les curés mêmes, au moment le plus menaçant, ont perdu l'habitude de gémir.[1]

In spite of the gloomy prognostications of the Right, the Separation and its aftermath did not provoke widespread disorders. The application of the law hardly affected the everyday lives of the great majority of Frenchmen.

Less than six months afterwards, housewives in the *beaux quartiers* of Paris were buying stores of non-perishable foods in preparation for a state of seige. Labour Day, 1906 was expected to be a revolutionary *journée* for the future of the bourgeois society was in doubt.

Clemenceau, the minister of the Interior, called up troops from the provinces and discovered a "plot" in which the leaders of the Confédération Général du Travail and certain members of the extreme extra-parliamentary Right were supposed to be planning revolutionary disturbances throughout the country.[2]

[1] Letter of Denys Cochin to Mme Pierre d'Harcourt, dated December 1905. Cochin MSS.

[2] Clemenceau wanted to implicate Jacques Piou, the president of Action libérale populaire in the plot but opposition within the cabinet prevented this. A charge was made by a Socialist in the Chamber that local branches of A.L.P. were involved. It is unlikely that Piou and the association which he led would have been a party to this kind of adventure. All charges against those who were alleged to have taken part in this plot were dropped in July 1906 when the Chamber passed an amnesty bill.

May Day passed without serious trouble but the *grand'peur* of the bourgeoisie remained. It was not without foundation. During the period 1906 to 1911, on different occasions, Paris was plunged into darkness, building stopped, coal ran short, trains ceased to run and civil servants went on strike. Strikers and members of the police and the army were injured and killed. All this was accompanied by a commentary of revolutionary pronouncements by trade union leaders in a period of comparative prosperity and progressive *embourgeoisement* of French society.

Social disturbances and renewed pressure for social and financial reforms, which had been delayed by the anti-clerical struggle, caused the replacement of "clericalism" by the "social problem" as the dominant issue in parliament almost as soon as the law of Separation was passed. But until 1914 parliamentarians were constantly reminded of the existence of the clerical issue. The line between clerical and anti-clerical remained the most obvious division in politics. Those who had opposed *combiste* policies and the law of Separation were tarred for the remainder of their political careers with the brush of clericalism.

This division was not without relevance in the great debate on the social problem because in a confused and general way the debate on the place of the Church in society was concerned with the privileges of classes and institutions. The non-Catholic, Progressiste and Nationalist, elements of the Right defended the Church as a social and not as a religious institution. The extreme Right and the extreme Left were equally convinced that the attack on the Church was part and parcel of the attack on private property. Three institutions, wrote Jules Delahaye, the most violent of the polemicists of the extreme Right in parliament, barred the route to the Red Republic towards which France was rapidly moving; these were religion, the family and private property – an attack on one of them was an attack on them all.[3] A less extreme man, Jacques Piou, declared that the defence of Christianity was equivalent to the defence of the "social order".[4] But in making these statements, the polemicists of the Right were either bidding in a tendentious manner for electoral support or they were blinded by their antipathies. The Radicals and the men of the Centre party, Alliance Démocratique, had as little desire to see a socialist state as the Right.

Between the Right and the Centre there was much common ground.

[3] *L'Autorité*, June 8, 1908.
[4] *Annuaire de l'Action libérale populaire . . . 1904–1905* (1904), p. 192.

Both desired the preservation of the institution of private property, order in the street and discipline in the factory. They desired a deferential working class which looked to them for moral, intellectual and political leadership. As long as the Right remained an isolated opposition as a result of the persisting importance of the clerical issue, this common ground was not apparent. Also at the beginning of the period different sections of the Right proposed very different, and sometimes mutually exclusive, tactics and methods to achieve social harmony. They contrasted with the more cautious and negative views of the Centre.

The purpose of this study is to relate the changing alignments in the Chamber and in the country between 1905 and 1919 to the all-pervasive influence of the social problem. As a background to these changes some discussion is necessary of the personal and constituency interests of the deputies, their general attitudes to the social problem and the positions they adopted on important social reforms. The Right was a diverse collection of men and any attempt to categorize and generalize about them necessarily involves simplification. The subject is so complex that some sacrifice of precision is inevitable.

II

In 1905, the term la Droite was properly applied only to the monarchists but it was used by the anticlerical majority in the Chamber to describe those groups which opposed the Separation.[5] It is used in this study in the same way. In 1905 the total strength of this opposition of the Right in the Chamber was 245. It was divided into five groups – Union Républicaine (U.R.), Républicain Progressiste (R.P.), Action Libérale (A.L.), Républicain Nationaliste (R.N.), and the unorganized Independents (Ind.). Until 1910 deputies were often members of more than one group. A change in the standing orders of the Chamber caused the publication of the group lists (each deputy could only appear on one list) in the *Journal officiel*. The practice of *double appartenance* ceased for a time. This change resulted in the temporary suppression of the Union Républicaine, the revival of the monarchist Groupe des Droites (Dr.)

[5] The socialists sometimes said, after 1905, that they regarded the Right as much more extensive than this. On the other hand, the *Journal officiel* described the Progressistes as the Centre and the Progressistes themselves declared that all Republicans were "forcement de gauche".

and the formation of the Groupe des Indépendants (Ind.). The Nationalist group disappeared after its members had suffered two severe electoral setbacks. The changes brought about by the elections of 1914 were the final disappearance of the Union Républicaine and the change of name of the Groupe Républicain Progressiste to the Fédération Républicaine. After the elections of 1919 the former members of the Fédération Républicaine and Action Liberale combined with some of the Indépendants, former members of Centre groups and many new deputies to form the Entente Républicaine Démocratique (E.R.D.). Monarchists, extremists and eccentrics made up two groups of independents.

The numerical representation of the Right declined rapidly between 1905 and 1919. The election of 1906 reduced its strength from 244 to 184. In 1910 there were 154 members of the groups of the Right, in 1914, 123 and only 64 of these survived the elections of 1919.[6] As well as being a declining opposition, the Right tended to be an ageing opposition. This was particularly noticeable on the extreme Right. The average age of the monarchist group in 1914 was 60·8. The average length of the parliamentary career of the survivors of the 1919 election was fourteen years compared with the average of 8·8 years of the deputies of the Right in 1905. Electoral defeat was not the only cause: the younger deputies tended to move leftwards in group membership after each general election.[7]

The five groups of the Right in 1905 had come into being at different

[6] The membership figures of the groups between 1905 and 1919 were these:

	1905	1906–10	1910–14	1914–19	1920
U.R.	30	46–47	0–29	—	—
R.P.	101	79–76	80–42	37–33	—
A.L.	79	64–59	34–31	24–20	—
R.N.	55	29–29	—	—	—
Dr.	—	—	19–20	16–12	—
Ind.	42	34–35	21–19	46–36	29
E.R.D.	—	—	—	—	186
Non-inscrits	—	—	—	—	26

The total number of deputies of the Right is exaggerated in the period 1905–10 because deputies with *double appartenance* are counted twice.

[7] This reflects the unimportance of the groups as organizations – deputies were not elected as members of a group (the electoral organizations were quite separate from the parliamentary groups). In spite of this group membership gives a fairly accurate guide to a deputy's political views.

times and in different circumstances. They had little in common except their antipathies. The Progressistes, in the days of the ascendancy of the moderate Republicans, had formed a part of the large amorphous section of the Chamber called the Républicains de Gouvernement. Since 1899 the growing power and militancy of the Radicals had forced them into opposition. The majority were not Catholics but they disliked intensely the kind of anticlericalism represented by Combes. The moderate wing of the Progressistes, led in 1905 by Joseph Thierry, found an opposition role uncongenial. The moderates as well as being members of the Républicain Progressiste group, were usually members of the Groupe de l'Union Républicaine, the *raison d'être* of which was to preserve contact with the Centre. The right wing of the Progressistes, notably Jules Méline and Jules Roche, came to have much in common with the rest of the Right and seemed to want to maintain the breach between themselves and the moderate Republicans of the Centre such as Poincaré, Leygues and Barthou.

The Liberals were the ralliés discussed by Mr. Shapiro in his article. They had changed the name of their parliamentary group in 1899 from Droite Républicaine to Action Libérale. In 1902 under the leadership of Piou and with Albert de Mun as vice-president, Action Libérale Populaire was founded in order to mobilize support in the country. This rapidly became a powerful organization, supported by a large section of the clergy and the approval of Rome, with a number of useful fringe organizations produced by the corporative tendencies within Catholicism. The Liberals hoped to become the nucleus of a large conservative party. This hope was destroyed by successive electoral defeats and by the guerilla war carried on by ultra-Catholics against the association.

The nationalist movement was produced by a reaction to the Dreyfusard campaign. Not in origin clericals, the Nationalists came to defend the Church as a great national institution against the attacks of their Dreyfusard enemies.[8] Conservatives, as Mr. Watson has shown, seized on nationalism as a useful electoral formula. By 1905 about half the parliamentary group were ex-monarchists. The nationalist movement declined, as it had risen, with the Dreyfusard campaign.

The Independents were an assorted collection of people, the most numerous group amongst them were the monarchists who ranged from

[8] There were still three anti-clerical nationalists in the Chamber in 1905 – Gabriel Failliot, Ernest Roche and Henri Tournade – who all represented constituencies in Paris. Only Tournade survived the election of 1906.

the urbane and liberal Denys Cochin to the intransigent marquis de Baudry d'Asson and included the scurrilous and ill-mannered Jules Delahaye. Other Independents were Jules Lemire, the abbé démocrate, Maurice Barrès, the most distinguished nationalist of the time, and in 1906, Pierre Biétry the organiser of "yellow" trade unions.

The political origins of the groups of the Right are easily identifiable. Their social bases are less so. No significant section of the economy was exclusively represented by a group of the Right or, indeed, by the Right as a whole. Only one extensive region of France – the West – was dominated by the Right. The personal interests of deputies of the Right and the interests of the constituencies which they represented were many and varied. They do not present us with a facile explanation of the political behaviour and attitudes of the Right.

Among the deputies of the Right there was a strong contingent from the land-owning, farming, army-officer class.[9] Its proportionate strength increased slightly (from 44·5 per cent in 1905 to 47·1 per cent at the beginning of 1919) as the Right declined. As one would expect, the extreme Right was more involved in these activities than the moderate Right – in 1905, 31 per cent of Union Républicaine as against 53 per cent of the Independents. The comparison is even more striking if only those whose interests were primarily landowning or farming are counted. Of the extreme Right, the monarchists were the most heavily biased towards the land; in 1910 89·3 per cent of the Groupe des Droites came within this category. The Liberals by 1914 had become dominated by the agricultural interest. Many of the landowners and farmers were active in agricultural affairs and drew their political strength and reputation from these activities. Perhaps the best known of these was Hyacinthe de Gailhard-Bancel (A.L.),

---

[9] The main sources used for discovering the personal interests of deputies can be found in the bibliography of collective biography at the end of this volume. Other indications have been found in autobiographies, biographies, electoral brochures, newspapers and miscellaneous writings on politics. Conversations with the late Adrien Thierry (son of Joseph Thierry), M. le colonel Philippe d'Elissagaray (son of Renaud d'Elissagaray) and M. Victor Bucaille (former secretary of Denys Cochin), have thrown additional light on the personal activities of the deputies of the Right. But classifications are necessarily arbitrary and subjective. For example, every member of the Right was probably a *propriétaire* in some sense but landowners are so-called only when there is evidence that they gained substantial revenues from land or if they had no other ascertainable form of income. The evidence to include or exclude deputies, especially the more obscure ones, from certain categories is sometimes meagre. Only the most important categories are mentioned.

deputy of Ardèche from 1898 to 1924, who pioneered agricultural unions in the Midi after the passing of the law of Associations of 1884.[10]

The deputies who had held commissions in the armed forces (16·2 per cent of the Right in 1905) were nearly all landowners or farmers. The exceptions were Henri Tournade (R.N.), deputy for Paris, who was Paris agent for the Peninsular and Orient line and Camille Fouquet (Ind.), deputy for Eure, who owned a manufacturing concern at Bernay. In 1905 Action Libérale had the highest proportion of ex-officers (22·8 per cent), in 1914 Fédération Républicaine (13·5 per cent) but the general pattern was that the extreme Right attracted more ex-officers and many of these were ex-cavalry officers.

The reverse pattern was apparent amongst the men involved in banking, commerce and industry – 21·6 per cent of the Right in 1905 and 15·6 per cent in 1914. After the elections of 1906, 43·5 per cent of the members of Union Républicaine as compared with 6·9 per cent of the Nationalist group were engaged in these activities. The moderate Right maintained its leadership throughout the period. The industrial interests of members of the Right were extremely varied. Amongst the industrialists on the Right were Eugène Schneider (A.L.), *maître des forges* and armament manufacturer, director of the famous Creusot works; the marquis de Dion (R.N.), founder and owner of the de Dion car works; Victor Vion (U.R.) president of a large sugar-beet manufacturing concern in Somme; Paul Lebaudy (U.R./R.P.) competed with him in cane-sugar refining; Armand Cardon (Ind.), Jules Dansette (A.L.) and Eugène Motte (R.P.) were involved in textile manufacturing in Nord; Edgar Laroche-Joubert (Ind.) was a paper manufacturer in Angers; Félix Leglise (U.R./R.P.) was owner of forests and lumber mills in Landes; and Gauthier de Clagny (R.N.) was a speculative builder (he developed the parc de Clagny in Versailles which had been the property of Mme de Montespan) and owner of a marble quarry. The interests of those engaged in commerce were also varied but there was a compact group of Progressiste free-traders whose constituencies lay in the large commercial centres of France – Edouard Aynard of Lyon, André Ballande of Bordeaux, Louis Brindeau of Le Havre, Paul Beauregard of Paris and Joseph Thierry of Marseilles. Although they did not deny their laissez-faire convictions,

[10] See H. de Gailhard-Bancel, *Les Syndicates agricoles aux champs et au parlement, 1884–1924* (1924). He was also the author of two brochures on syndical activity.

they had become reconciled to a protectionist world. They favoured commercial treaties and were cautious imperialists. Thierry, Brindeau and Ballande were especially concerned with colonial trade.[11] However, most Progressistes under the leadership of Méline were resolutely protectionist in matters of international trade.

The bankers of the Right had extensive interests outside banking and usually had connections with the Banque de France – Guy de Wendel (elected 1914; Ind.) was *maître des forges* and a regent of the Banque de France; Edouard Aynard (R.P.) was a silk manufacturer, a director of many industrial concerns in the Lyon area and agent of the Bank; Ballande directed a shipping and trading house in Bordeaux and was a *censeur* of the Bank. The only exception to this combination was Raphael Bischoffshiem (R.P.) an immensely rich merchant banker who originally came from Amsterdam. He had been naturalized by presidential decree after making large gifts to French scientific establishments. From 1889 to 1906 he was deputy for Nice, but he never spoke in the Chamber.

Fewer deputies of the extreme Right than of the moderate Right had been civil servants or had been law officers holding government appointments. This reflected the longer period that most of the extreme Right had spent in political opposition. There were only three surviving servants of Napoleon III still in the Chamber – baron Armand Mackau (A.L.), Arthur Legrand (Ind.) and Gaston Galpin (Ind.). As the years passed the proportion of civil servants and law officers in the Right as a whole dropped (from 11·8 per cent in 1905 to 8·4 per cent in 1914) which merely showed that more members of the Right had spent their adult lives in political opposition. A number of members of the Right had had highly successful careers in government service. François Arago retired from the diplomatic corps with the title of *ministre plénipotentiaire*; the marquis de Chambrun (R.P.) had been ambassador of France to Washington. Louis Andrieux (Ind.) had been prefect of Police in the eighties; Henry Lozé (R.P.) held this post later in the same decade. There were five former *sous-préfets*.

A few of the Right had held office in governments – (Godefroy Cavaignac (R.N.), Emile Flourens (R.N.), Louis Passy (A.L.), Alex-

[11] At this time, apart from those engaged in the colonial trade, only Prosper Ancel Seitz (Ind.), deputy for Vosges, who possessed estates in the French Congo, had a large financial stake in the colonies. The interest of the Right in the Empire came mainly through personal relations with those of the army officer class who had served in the colonies.

andre Ribot (R.P.) and Jules Roche (R.P.)) but not enough to give the impression of an alternative administration. There were seven Progressistes who subsequently became ministers, most of them in the period 1919–24. One of them, Albert Lebrun, was the last President of the Third Republic.

The traditional avenues into politics, law and journalism, were practised extensively by members of the Right although to a lesser degree than by members of the Centre and Left. In 1905 just over a quarter of the deputies of the Right had been practising lawyers, either as *avocats, avoués* or *notaires* and the proportion tended to rise slightly. In spite of the reputation which the Right had for being inarticulate, nearly all deputies contributed fairly regularly to their local paper and there was a high proportion – 11·8 per cent in 1905 and 20·6 per cent in 1914 – of serious journalists. Few of the latter can have made much money out of journalism or any other form of writing. A notable exception was the novelist and journalist, Maurice Barrès, who bought the château of Mirabeau in 1906 from the proceeds of his writing. Others, such as Albert de Mun (A.L.), Charles Benoist (R.P.) and Jules Delafosse (Ind.) gained fame, if not fortune, through their pens. There were notable newspaper editors on the Right – François Arago of *le Petit Journal*, Paul Beauregard (R.P.), founder and editor of *le Monde économique*, Jules Roche (R.P.), editor from 1906 to 1910 of *la République française* and Georges Bonnefous (R.P.), editor from 1900 to 1905 of *l'Année politique* – (he helped to revive it after the second world war). Anthime Ménard (R.P.) was probably the most influential provincial journalist. He founded *l'Observateur* (1878) and *la Nouvelliste de l'Ouest* (1891) which became a focal point for the ralliement in the West.

The constituency interests of the Right can only be discussed in general terms. The distribution of the constituencies of the Right during the period 1905 to 1919 was wide. Only fifteen departments sent no representative of the Right to the Palais Bourbon. Six of these formed a contiguous unit in the Centre of France.[12] This barren area was usually much more extensive – it comprised eleven departments in 1914.[13] The Right was in general poorly represented in the Eastern departments (with the exception of Vosges and Meurthe et Moselle) and by 1914 representation had dwindled to almost nothing in the

[12] Allier, Cher, Corrèze, Creuse, Loir et Cher, Haute Vienne.
[13] In addition to those in note 12: Cantal, Dordogne, Nièvre, Puy de Dôme, Yonne.

south-east. These regions were, by and large, opposed to change but they voted Centre Republican rather than Right.

The main electoral strongholds of the Right were the West, the North (especially Nord and Pas de Calais) and greater Paris, which together formed a total of twenty departments. The south-west was an unstable fourth bastion. The West was the most important stronghold of the Right. In 1905, sixty-seven deputies of the Right came from twelve Western departments.[14] As the overall total of deputies of the Right fell the proportion of those coming from the West rose. These departments were largely rural, poor and Catholic. The prestige of the priest and *châtelain* survived as a major social force. The economic and social changes which had taken place in the rest of France since the Revolution were alien to this society if not directly hostile to it.

The persistence of Catholicism and the benevolent paternalism of the *patronat* had preserved the political strength of the Right in Nord and Pas de Calais. But the effectiveness of these forces was waning. In 1905 twenty deputies of the Right came from these departments, in 1914 there were eight. In 1919 (under the *scrutin de liste*), a socialist list came top of the poll in Nord, another socialist list won all the seats in the first constituency of Pas de Calais and in the other, more rural, constituency, the Right had to make an alliance with radical socialists in order to gain representation.

In Seine the elections of 1906 reduced the representation of the Right from twenty-three (fifteen of whom belonged to the Nationalist group in the Chamber) to fifteen (only five of whom joined the Nationalist group). The Right revived a little in the capital – it had eighteen deputies in 1914. In 1919, the victory of the national lists in three out of the four constituencies of Paris was not a victory for the Right. Only six outgoing deputies of the Right were re-elected and seven notable *anciens députés* – Bienaimé (Ind.), Denais (A.L.), Failliot (Ind.), Lerolle (A.L.), Pugliesi-Conti (Ind.), Spronck (F.R.), and Tournade (F.R.) – were defeated. The representation of the Right in Seine-et-Oise declined from eight to two in the period 1905 to 1919.

The different tendencies within the Right had some regional attachments. The Nationalists were concentrated in Paris and the West (mainly in constituencies with an urban element) with a few in the south-west (d'Elissagaray, Jacquey). Monarchists came mainly from the West but there were a couple of surviving *blancs du Midi*. The

[14] Calvados, Côtes du Nord, Finistère, Ille et Vilaine, Loire Inférieure, Maine et Loire, Manche, Mayenne, Morbihan, Orne, Sarthe, Vendée.

Liberals were hardly represented at all in Paris, they were comparatively strong in the North and West and they held some of the formerly monarchists seats in the South (Piou, Gailhard-Bancel). The Progressistes were the most widely and evenly distributed. They held seats in all the areas, both rural and urban, where the Right was represented.

The constituencies of the Right fell within three general categories. The first, the predominantly agricultural, included most of the constituencies held by the Right. There was a considerable variation in the social structure of agricultural society in different regions of France and consequently the political allegiance of their inhabitants differed. Agricultural constituencies elected deputies of nearly all the tendencies represented in parliament. They provided deputies for all the groups of the Right in the Chamber. At first sight the agricultural interest appears to have alarming electoral strength, but as a result of political division and more especially because the interests of the various agricultural activities seldom coincide, it rarely acted as a united pressure group.

The second category was the traditional industrial, that is areas which were still dominated by family firms. The Right benefited here from both the Catholic and the deferential vote. The North was the only significant area in this category and the constituencies in which the Right was strongest in that region were, in general, partly agricultural. The third category was the urban commercial. Constituencies of this type were usually found in certain quarters of all the large cities. If they voted Right, they returned Nationalists or Progressistes. The only exception was the first constituency of the eighth arrondissement of Paris which elected Denys Cochin.[15] In 1905, the material interests of these constituencies had not been gravely disturbed by the governments of the *bloc des gauches*. They were alarmed by what these governments were about to do and what they might do rather than what they had done.

[15] The only categories missing were the provincial towns (where constituency boundaries were not drawn to include large areas of countryside) and the modern, urban industrial. The Right captured a seat with an urban working-class majority when Pierre Biétry defeated the Socialist Goude in Brest in 1906. But the candidate and the circumstances were exceptional.

III

There was a variety of views held by members of the Right in 1905 concerning the general causes and remedies for the social problem. These general attitudes were amalgams and vulgarizations of the ideas of celebrated and of obscure theorists. They were formed over a long period of time and although modified by circumstances, the changes were never dramatic and seldom even apparent. The formation, transmission and modification of the traditional attitudes of the Right concerning the social problem are not within the scope of this paper. But it is important to realize that views on the social problem were not necessarily made up to meet a particular situation.

The great majority of the Right in 1905 approached the problem with a few simple prejudices about their opponents. They disliked and distrusted working-class organizations. The Bourses du Travail, the C.G.T. and the more militant unions were regarded with a deep antipathy and were not considered representative of the working-class. Just as many elements of the Right thought that the anticlerical agitation was the result of a masonic-jewish-protestant conspiracy, so also they thought that anarchists, syndicalists, some Radicals, Socialists and assorted criminals were together plotting the overthrow of society. Many members of the Right also seemed to think that "the Revolution" was imminent.

The Progressistes were the most negative section of the Right in their attitudes to the social problem. An opponent wrote that it was they who organized opposition in the country to "l'établissement des relations plus démocratiques entre le capital et le travail par l'intervention de l'Etat".[16] Much more than the Liberal or the extreme Right they defended the economic status quo and they sometimes said that the real division in politics was not between monarchist and republican nor clerical and anticlerical but between socialist and anti-socialist.[17] They invoked, without much logic or consistency, the principles of the great Revolution to attack the social doctrines, the policies and the organizations of the Left. Liberty to Progressistes meant laissez-faire, although the majority of Progressiste deputies were partisans of protective tariffs. They tended to be alarmed by the most trivial

[16] A. Vasse, *Pour qui voter?* (1910), p. 29.
[17] E.g. Jules Roche in *la République française*, July 21, 1907; Joseph Thierry in *la Revue hebdomadaire*, March 26, 1910, p. 463.

legislation which interfered with entrepreneurial freedom in the interests of the working-class. Joseph Thierry, as president of the Fédération Républicaine, tried hard to make the party accept the inevitability and desirability of social reform. But in spite of his efforts – "Bourgeois, levez-vous, unissez-vous!" – the injudicious slogan which terminated an article in *la République française* (November 19, 1909) seemed more typical of the group than Thierry's reasonable words.

Two Progressiste deputies, Charles Benoist and Jules Méline, made systematic studies of the social problem[18] but their conclusions were no more (and perhaps even less) progressive than those of the majority of their colleagues. Benoist, after making an enquiry into five major industries, concluded that the crisis of the modern state was caused by the incompatibility of the society thrown up by the industrial revolution with the institutions of the country.[19] He thought that constitutional reform (his most famous campaign was for proportional representation) and the charitable efforts of private individuals were the only remedies for the social problem. He opposed interference in the free play of the market, even in the interests of grossly exploited young women.[20]

Jules Méline, senator for Vosges and an ex-prime minister, was at one time associated with the textile interest but by 1905 he had become primarily the spokesman of agricultural proprietors. His views fascinate by their very perversity. He considered that industrial production could not continue to expand at the current rate indefinitely:

> Nous n'allons pas jusqu'à dire que l'industrie descend, mais elle nous paraît tout au moins à son apogée pendant que l'agriculture monte visiblement.[21]

He argued that consumption of industrial goods must inevitably lag behind production – citing, quite irrelevantly, the periodic slump in the market for industrial goods and the phenomenal, and, to him, unnatural growth in the export trade. He prophesied that people would, through necessity, return to the land. Méline opposed social reforms on the grounds that interference in the economy by the

[18] An important group of Progressistes, Aynard, Beauregard, Leroy-Beaulieu and Roche, wrote and spoke frequently on the social problem but they were primarily concerned with the furtherance of conservative financial policies.

[19] Ch. Benoist, *La Crise de l'état moderne* (1905–14), 2 vols.

[20] Ch. Benoist, *Les Ouvrières de l'aiguille à Paris, notes pour l'étude de la question sociale* (1895).

[21] J. Méline, *Le Retour à la terre et la surproduction industrielle* (1905), p. 102.

"heavy hand" of the state would lead to economic disaster. Yet he advocated protective tariffs and extensive state support for agriculture. In some respects his thinking anticipated the autarkic assumptions of the inter-war period. His main appeal was to conservatives who were alarmed by the decline of rural society.

The Catholic Right was more positive in its approach to the social problem. A Catholic who expounded laissez-faire doctrines appeared disrespectful of papal teaching. Certain Catholics took the social teachings of the Church seriously and produced a steady trickle of reform proposals. Like Benoist (who became a monarchist after the first world war), the monarchists believed that the social problem was created by wrong doctrines about authority.[22] Liberty of association had become the keystone of monarchist doctrine, and the monarchist senator, Gustave de Lamarzelle, called for the creation of a new aristocracy based on the representatives of voluntary organizations.[23] Without powerful voluntary organizations to protect the liberty and material interests of their members, Lamarzelle considered that social legislation was merely a palliative and could not solve the problems of social frustration and unrest.

The great Liberal leader, Albert de Mun, was attached by upbringing and affection to the monarchist aristocracy. But unlike Lamarzelle he showed no faith that a new aristocracy could rise out of the ruins of the old. He was mainly concerned with the plight of the urban proletariat, which he had discovered during the suppression of the Paris commune.[24] By 1905 the famous *cercles ouvriers*, which he had founded to bring the bourgeoisie and the workers into contact, were all but defunct and his ideas had developed little since the programme of Saint Etienne (December 1892), but his views probably commanded wider assent amongst the Right than ever before. His social programme was a mixture of conservative formulae and claims for the poor. Although he approved of state assistance for and protection of the

[22] Official monarchist doctrine (which was vague) was defined by the pretender. See *La Monarchie française; lettres et documents politiques, 1844-1907* (1907), Especially pp. 14–16, 261.

[23] G. de Lamarzelle, *Démocratie politique, démocratie sociale, démocratie chrétienne* (1907). Especially pp. 26–35. The uncompromising defenders of the old aristocracy argued that moral qualities (which the representatives of the new industrial, commercial and professional corporations did not possess) gave it the right to rule. See for example, the pamphlet of the monarchist senator, Emmanuel de Las Cases, *Les Autorités sociales dans une démocratie* (1903).

[24] See A. de Mun, *Ma Vocation sociale* (1908).

poor, he preferred private initiative whenever possible. He wanted encouragement for friendly societies and was impressed by the growth of syndical organization since the law of Associations of 1884.[25] He did not like many of the social reforms proposed by the Left but was prepared to accept some of them, such as the obligatory old age pension scheme, as being better than nothing.

Action Libérale Populaire (de Mun was vice-president) was the only party of the Right which attempted to formulate a precise social programme. Corporatism was the basis of this programme. The local branches of the association were encouraged to set up study groups, "secrétariats du peuple, mutualités, cercles populaires, caisses de prêt, jardins ouvriers". A leading member of A.L.P., Hyacinth de Gailhard-Bancel, proposed that professional associations should be encouraged by legislation and that official consultative machinery should be set up.[26] Piou, the president of A.L.P., said that it was difficult to ameliorate social hardship by voluntary action and by legislative reform because of the prevalence of evil doctrines – reconversion to Christianity was the final solution to the social problem.[27]

Coming as they did mainly from rural areas, many members of A.L.P. were ready to admit that the wages of the industrial proletariat were far too low. They occasionally made polemics against the power of money and high finance. But on agricultural matters they were much more conservative. The association was, for example, opposed to the extension to agricultural workers of obligatory accident insurance.[28] Rural depopulation was attributed to the waning influence of the *autorités sociales* and the rural bourgeoisie.[29]

The Christian Democrats, represented in parliament by the abbés Gayraud (A.L.) and Lemire (Ind.), were in their political attitudes, the most leftist of the Catholics.[30] Gayraud was the theorist. But on social

[25] He came to accept the class nature of this development. Letter to Association catholique de la jeunesse française, May 10, 1903.

[26] G. Maze-Sencier, *L'Amélioration du sort des travailleurs* (1906). Preface by H. de Gailhard-Bancel, p. iv.

[27] *Congrès social de Pau. Compte rendu* (Pau, 1903), p. 224.

[28] *Annuaire de l'Action libérale populaire . . . 1904–1905* (1904), p. 191.

[29] G. Maze-Sencier, *Les Cahiers agricoles de l'Action libérale populaire* (Mende, 1909), pp. 25, 61 ff.

[30] A Christian democratic party had been formed in 1897, the prime movers of which were the abbés, Naudet, Dabry, Lemire and Gayraud. This party dissociated itself from all conservative Catholic political groups. However, the anticlerical agitation frustrated any attempt at co-operation with the Left.

THE RIGHT AND THE SOCIAL QUESTION IN PARLIAMENT

matters his first concerns were the traditional conservative preoccupations – "la religion, la famille et la propriété privée". He advocated, on the grounds of Christian principle, a more equitable distribution of wealth but never discussed in detail how this was to be achieved. The abuses of the existing order resulted from "machinisme" (enslavement to machines) and usury. Jews and usury were closely connected in his mind (he suggested measures to regulate both) and this, to a certain extent, identified him with the extreme Right.[31] Lemire was a man of action who concerned himself with limited practical reforms. His most successful venture was the Ligue du Coin de Terre et du Foyer, the main purpose of which was to procure allotments for working men. In the Chamber he was especially interested in legislation to protect the family. His conception of the family was traditional; he had no sympathy with feminism. There was little in the social views of Gayraud or Lemire to substantiate the claim (rarely made after the *combiste* anticlerical campaign had got under way) that they were men of the Left. They did, however, show more goodwill towards reforms proposed by the Left than the rest of the Right. Where they differed radically from their Catholic colleagues was in their rejection of the "social powers" as necessary supports for the Church and for any Catholic political organization.

On the extreme nationalist Right there was a confusion of views. Sometimes there was a rapprochement with the extreme Left. On occasion a member of the extreme Right would condemn the use of force during strikes and syndicalist riots and employers would be urged to make concession. But the other side of the coin was more frequently in view. There was always at least one member of the extreme Right to condemn the most innocuous social reform. For example, Jules Delahaye (Ind.) opposed the bill for a weekly day of rest, which was generally approved on the Right, calling it a Jewish thing.[32] Encouragement of black-leg workers and violent attacks on trade unions were much more frequent than expressions of sympathy and common interest. The only kind of protection for the workers which all members of the extreme Right supported was protection against competition from foreign workmen.

Most of the theoretical statements by members of the extreme Right on the social problem were deeply pessimistic.[33] An interesting

[31] Abbé Gayraud, *Les Démocrates chrétiens* (1899), pp. 14, 52–3, 62–3, 160, 199.
[32] *L'Autorité*, September 5, 1906.
[33] E.g. Jules Delahaye, *Théorie de l'autorité* (1899), pp. 361–97.

exception was Pierre Biétry, deputy for Brest (1906–10) and organizer of a group of black-leg unions – the Fédération des Jaunes – which was financed by industrialists. His ideas, although the most obvious plagiarisms, have some significance because of his activities. He called his doctrines, developed in two books and numerous articles,[34] "propriétisme";

> Les jaunes disent que les ouvriers et les paysans sont plus malheureux quand ils ne possèdent rien, et que ce n'est pas en leur faisant signer leur renonciation à la conquête de la propriété, c'est-à-dire en les rendant socialistes, qu'on les fera heureux, mais en les aidant à conquérir, à acquérir la propriété.[35]

He alleged that slaves had been emancipated and serfs enfranchised because they had come to own property and that all social progress resulted from the intimate co-operation of capital labour and intelligence. The main points of his programme were vigorous anti-socialism, property-ownership for the workers, compulsory unionization and the regional grouping of the unions, the improvement of the lot of the poor by private initiative, friendly societies and, in the last resort, by legislation. Biétry had a brief moment of glory but by 1914 his movement had almost completely disappeared.

The idiosyncratic attitudes held by members of the Right in 1905 were mainly attempts to justify or support, not the rights of property as such, but the rights of certain propertied classes, the most notable being the old aristocracy and the *bien pensant* bourgeoisie. The decline in wealth and power of these sections of the community made apparent the intellectual nakedness of the attempts to justify their pretensions to leadership. Important sections of the Right, such as Action libérale, no longer cared to formulate an overt justification. Much of the thinking of the Right on the social problem was not idiosyncratic; many of the attitudes expressed by Progressistes were shared by the Centre. These common attitudes became more and more important during the period 1905 to 1919, when, as a result of the increasing representation of the

---

[34] *Les Jaunes de France et la question ouvrière* (1906); *Le Socialisme et les jaunes* (1906); *Le Trépied* (1911). Biétry ran two newspapers – *La Jaune* (Paris) and *Le Genêt de Bretagne* (Brest) – as well as contributing to the other journals of the extreme Right.

[35] Part of the manifesto of the Jaunes to the Russian people. *L'Autorité*, August 29, 1907.

Socialists, it became obvious (except to certain diehard reactionaries) that all property owners, whether Radicals or Bonapartists, had common interests and they might have to co-operate to defend them. Consequently, there was a decline (particularly noticeable after 1911) in the amount of theorizing done by the Right, and in the frequency with which idiosyncratic views were expressed.

IV

The parliamentary Right was compelled to consider two different categories of issues connected with the social problem. The first was agitation by civil servants, railwaymen and others. The second was legislation designed to alleviate social distress, based on the principles of "welfare economics" and the effect of which was to achieve a small re-distribution of wealth, in the cases of old age pensions and income tax, and power in the community in the case of nationalization of the Western railway.

Since the breaking of the postmen's strike in 1899, successive governments had adopted a policy of laissez-aller on the right of civil servants to form unions. Those which were already in existence were recognized; new unions were neither recognized nor suppressed. Clemenceau, as minister of the Interior, reiterated this policy during an interpellation on April 12, 1906 concerning another postmen's strike.[36]

During this debate the speakers of the Right were hostile to the postmen's union and to the strike. But fourteen of the extreme Right, not displeased to see the inability of the government to control its own servants, voted against it. The postmen went on strike twice in the first half of 1909. Much sympathy was expressed for postmen by the extreme Right. The Marquis de Rosanbo (Ind.) said that the doctrines of Clemenceau and Briand were really responsible for their behaviour. Joseph Lasies (R.N.) thought that the misdemeanours of the government were far more serious than those of the postmen.[37] Jules Delahaye (Ind.) whilst opposing in principle the right of civil servants to strike, argued in favour of it in the existing state of affairs as being the post-

---

[36] For a description of the unions and government policy at this time see M. Leroy, *Les Transformations de la puissance publique* (1907), pp. 201–38.

[37] *J.O.*, March 19, 1909, pp. 783, 785.

men's only defence against injustices.[38] One eccentric, the Marquis de Baudry d'Asson (Ind.) supported the union and the strike:

> La liberté est due à tous, républicains, bonapartistes ou royalistes . . . Je vote donc pour les grèvistes toujours au nom de liberté. Je vote pour les grèvistes parce qu'au bout du compte j'ai applaudi leur mouvement.[39]

At the end of the debate on the second postmen's strike of 1909 only five members of the extreme Right voted in favour of the right of civil servants to strike. In other words, there were few who were prepared to pursue a *politique du pire*.

The postmen were the only non-industrial civil servants to go on strike during this period but the school teachers caused almost equal scandal by forming a union and affiliating to the C.G.T. During the debate on the government's counter-measures in May 1907, Alexandre Ribot (R.P.) presented the view of the majority of the Right and Joseph Massabuau (A.L.) the view of a significant minority on the position of civil servants. Ribot categorically denied the right of civil servants to bargain with the government and parliament. Although alleging that standards of ministerial behaviour had declined since he was in power, he did not regard this or any other reason advanced by civil servants as sufficient grounds for allowing them to form unions. He was not alarmed by the possibility of strikes because he did not think that civil servants were disposed to strike but he was concerned by the other forms of pressure which civil servants could bring to bear on government and parliament, especially at election time.[40]

Massabuau placed the responsibility for the discontent of the civil servants squarely on the shoulders of the ministers of the previous two decades. Civil servants, he said, would not feel the need for unions if they had always been treated justly and equitably. But since they wanted unions they should have them because the right of association was the very essence of democracy. Massabuau made a distinction, which more of his colleagues rejected, between higher and lower civil servants, drawing an analogy between the latter and the industrial

---

[38] *J.O.*, May 13, 1909, p. 1031. Even those who argued, like Gauthier de Clagny (R.N.) and Jules Dansette (A.L.), (*J.O.* March 19, 1909), against the strike on practical grounds, e.g. its effects on the economy – were sympathetic to the postmen.

[39] *J.O.*, May 13, 1909, p. 1031.

[40] *J.O.*, May 14, 1907. Especially pp. 990–2.

employees of the state (whose right to strike was not contested). He thought that higher civil servants should have separate associations and should not have the right to strike.[41] Massabuau and certain nationalists – notably Barrès, Gauthier de Clagny, Lasies, Millevoye and Tournade – voted for an order of the day asking the government to show good-will towards the school teachers and a majority of the Right refused to vote confidence in the government's policy.[42]

The Right, as a whole, had an ambivalent attitude towards civil servants. It regarded them as parasitic, as representatives of bureau-cratic tyranny, as political agents of the *bloc des gauches* and, in the case of the school teachers, as purveyors of unhealthy doctrines. But it clearly wished to blame the sins of the civil servants on their political masters and also to take advantage of their discontents. There was therefore a considerable amount of sympathy expressed for the civil servants in spite of the authoritarian instincts of the Right and the general feeling that public servants should not hold the community up to ransom.

This latter attitude coloured the views of the Right on strike action taken by railwaymen. Many members of the Right thought that the railways were an essential national service. During the debate in the Chamber on the railway strike of October 1910, a Progressiste, Paul Beauregard, a Liberal, Amédée Reille, and a Monarchist, Fernand de Ramel all affirmed their belief that the railwaymen's right to form unions did not necessarily imply the right to strike. All except three of the Right approved the action of Briand in breaking the strike by mobilizing the strikers.

In fact little opposition came from the Right when the government intervened against strikers in any other part of the private sector of the economy. When Clemenceau threatened to call in the army to replace striking electricians only two members of the Right, Joseph Lasies (R.N.) and the Marquis de Pins (R.N.), voted for a hostile order of the day (March 11, 1907). Joseph Thierry (R.P.), the only orator of the Right to speak, praised the government's intervention in the seamen's strike of April–May 1910 during which the government had refused to recognize the seamen's union and had given orders that the strikers should be tried for desertion. Since protection of the French workman against foreign competition had been a perennial item on the nationalist

[41] *J.O.*, May 8, 1907. Especially pp. 933–4.
[42] Over half – 118 – the opposing votes to the Maujan (*Rad. Soc.*) order of the day, May 14, 1907, which was carried by 323 votes to 205, came from the Right.

programme, some of the extreme Right voted against the government on this occasion as the seamen complained that foreigners were being employed on French ships at very low wages.

Sometimes there were criticisms from the Right that the government did not intervene actively enough in certain industrial disputes. This was the complaint of Joseph Lasies (R.N.) about the government's policy over the strike which followed the mining disaster of Currières in March 1906.[43] Georges Berry (R.N.) roundly condemned the government for not intervening to put a stop to the lock-out by the building firms in 1908 which was causing hardship in his constituency.[44]

The Right showed its limited sympathy for the working class by favouring amnesty proposals for those disciplined during strikes. In July 1906, during the discussion of the amnesty bill for those arrested for complicity in the May Day disturbances, the extreme Left tried to extend the amnesty to postmen who had not been reinstated after the April strike. Maurice-Binder (A.L.) spoke strongly in favour of this. Although the Right was opposed to the amnesty for the conspirators of May because it wanted the government to produce its evidence for involving the extreme Right in the alleged plot, a significant number of the more extreme half of the Right voted in favour of amnesty for the postmen.[45] The aftermath of the serious disturbances at Draveil-Vigneux (Seine-et-Oise) in 1908 provoked another amnesty debate. Jean Argeliès (U.R./R.P.), who represented the area in which the disturbances had taken place, proposed an amnesty bill for those who still remained in prison. He argued that they were not the real instigators of the disturbances (several prominent members of the C.G.T. had been arrested but subsequently released) and that an amnesty would help general social *apaisement*. A majority of the Right voted for this bill – the extreme Right were much more favourable to the bill

---

[43] *J.O.*, April 3, 1906, p. 542.

[44] *J.O.*, April 10, 1908. On the other hand, government intervention was sometimes thought to provoke violence. See, for example, Maurice Spronck (R.P.) in *la République française*, June 12, 1908, Jean Argeliès (U.R./R.P.) and the marquis de Rosanbo (Ind.). *J.O.*, June 11, 1908.

[45] The groups divided (counting twice those with *double appartenance*):

	FOR	AGAINST	ABSTENTIONS
U.R.	2	46	1
R.P.	4	70	2
A.L.	8	39	17
R.N.	14	9	4
Ind.	5	10	17

than were the moderate Right.[46] The extreme Right believed that the workers were led astray by a small clique of conspirators and it was they who should be punished, rather than their unfortunate, misguided followers caught by the authorities during riots. The Progressistes were also opposed to the leaders and demanded with equal force the suppression of the C.G.T.,[47] but they were less sympathetic to the rank and file and had fewer illusions about the nature of working-class agitation.

The breaking of the railway strike in October 1910, which underlined the limitations of the allegiance of rank and file unionists to their union, ended the period of strikes which had revolutionary overtones. At the height of the syndicalist agitation the differences between the majority of the Right and the majority of the Centre were of secondary importance – and solely about tactics. In the three years of comparative social peace, from 1911 to 1914, the views peculiar to the extreme Right were seldom heard. During and immediately after the war, the Right and Centre were in complete agreement that strike action was immoral and against the national interest. The strikes of 1917 and 1919 found the Right solidly behind the government. The *politique du pire*, never practised by more than a small minority of the Right over questions arising out of social disturbances, disappeared entirely.

There were much more serious differences of opinion on legislative proposals. The three major bills which achieved some redistribution of power and wealth – the nationalization of the Western railway, old age pension and income tax – were issues of principle almost on the level of the Separation of the Churches and the State. The Right was almost as united in opposing them.

The nationalization of the Western railway was the least important.

[46] The groups divided (counting twice those with *double appartenance*):

	FOR	AGAINST	ABSTENTIONS
U.R.	4	32	5
R.P.	26	34	4
A.L.	48	4	6
R.N.	26	2	–
Ind.	28	3	3

[47] Jules Roche (R.P.), Gauthier de Clagny (R.N.), and Pièrre Biétry (Ind.) signed a collective demand for the suppression of the C.G.T. *La Presse*, May 18, 1907. There were often articles by Progressiste deputies demanding either measures against, or suppression of the C.G.T. For example, Paul Beauregard and Maurice Spronck in *la République française*, May 10, 1907, February 7, 1908.

Large state subsidies had been necessary since the company began operating to meet running costs and the guaranteed rates of interest to the shareholders. There had long been a demand for *rachat* or nationalization on the grounds that it was unreasonable for the taxpayer to subsidize a private company indefinitely. This was not a revolutionary demand as the state had reserved the right in the original conventions with the railway companies to buy out the shareholders if this became necessary. It was pointed out (by Louis Barthou) in the debate in 1906 that the advocates of state railways were not necessarily men of the Left and that conservative governments had nationalized railways.

The Clemenceau government proposed a nationalization bill and pushed it through the Chamber with a speed which the Right considered was alarming.[48] The bill had only one article stating the principle of nationalization and there was little well-established information on the financial implications of the measure. *Le Temps* (December 9, 1906) described it as "une œuvre à la fois économique et politique" and the Right condemned it in both of these aspects. One frequently expressed opinion was that the bill was "un apéritif" opening the door to further interventions of the state in the economy[49] and even to the confiscation of property.[50] But as Louis Cachet (A.L./R.N.) pointed out, it was a poor starting point for a general reorganization of society. Unwisely, the Right concentrated mainly on the alleged political nature of the measure. Paul Beauregard (R.P.) stated that the measure was essentially and perhaps solely political:

... c'est parce que le parti qui a approuvé la Séparation des Eglises et de l'Etat a triomphé que l'on vous demande de racheter l'Ouest.[51]

Savary de Beauregard (A.L.) said that although he approved the principle of a state-owned railway he opposed this nationalization because it was motivated by political considerations. By interpreting it as a sanction taken by the *bloc des gauches* against the Catholic, conservative society of the West and one designed to increase the electoral influence of the *bloc* in that region, the Right united its enemies. Those who voted

---

[48] Paul Beauregard (R.P.), *la République française*, December 19, 1906. Jean Plichon (A.L.), *J.O.*, December 6, 1906, p. 2939. The debate lasted three days.

[49] Ferdinand Farjon (R.P.), *J.O.*, December 5, 1906, p. 2917. Jean Plichon (A.L.), *J.O.*, December 6, 1906, p. 2939.

[50] Louis Ollivier (A.L.), *J.O.*, December 7, 1906, p. 3010.

[51] *J.O.*, December 6, 1906, p. 2949; December 7, 1906, pp. 2971, 2978.

against the measure were not primarily those who opposed it on economic grounds.[52] It was an extended regional opposition.

The vote of the Chamber stimulated the opposition press campaign and opposition was rapidly organized in the Senate. This was given a great filip by the election of a *rapporteur*, hostile to the bill, for the committee set up to examine it. The committee then proceeded to hear representatives of the commercial interests of the West who, for the most part, were opposed to the bill. Nearly two years after the Chamber's vote the committee presented a hostile report. Although Charles Prevet (R.P.), the *rapporteur*, said that the population and the economic interests of the West were opposed to the bill, his main arguments were concerned with the cost of the measure to the taxpayer[53]. He received powerful support from the Radical ex-ministers, Rouvier and Viger. The clerical Right limited itself to brief interruptions and although the old argument that the nationalization was "un coup de main sur les départements de l'opposition"[54] was repeated by the press of the Right, it played little part in the Senate debate. The government came near to defeat when it made the rejection of a motion of adjournment proposed by the committee a matter of confidence.[55] The principle of nationalization was passed on June 26, 1908, only after the government had conceded that the procedure of nationalization and the subsequent running of the railway should be subject to special legislation. This delayed the application of the measure and prevented a precedent being created for the organization of nationalized industries by administrative degree. The difficulty which the government had in getting the measure through the Senate was the result of the opposition of economically conservative radicals. This opposition might have also been apparent in the Chamber if the Right had modified its tactics. Dislike of the principle of nationalization was not restricted to the Right as the vote of the Chamber seemed to suggest.

The delaying action fought by the opponents of a national system of pensions was impressive. The Chamber debated a scheme in every year of the decade 1891–1901 but did not pass a bill until 1906 and, as a result of senatorial obstruction, no scheme was in effective operation

[52] It was voted on December 7, 1906, by 364 votes to 187. Nine members of the groups of the Right voted for it – 3 U.R., 3 U.R./R.P., 2 R.P., 1 Ind.; twenty of the Centre voted against.
[53] *J.O., Sénat*, June 5, 1908, pp. 717 ff.
[54] *L'Autorité*, June 17, 1908.
[55] The government majority was only three. June 25, 1908.

before the first world war. Until 1906 the Right was opposed to an obligatory pension scheme but after the bill passed the Chamber there were important defections from this opposition.

A number of amendments, proposed by members of the Right when the bill was before the Chamber, were designed to weaken the principle of obligatory participation. The last, proposed by Henri Groussau (A.L.), was very nearly successful. This amendment proposed privileges for privately endowed pension schemes. Groussau appealed openly to paternalist instincts[56] and his proposal rallied all those who preferred private initiative to state intervention to ameliorate social hardship. They included all the Right and many members of the Centre, particularly those who had interests in friendly societies. The amendment was defeated by 278 votes to 257. It was the last stand of the opposition in the Chamber.

The campaign against the pension bill continued. Jules Roche stumped the country making speeches in which he condemned it as a socialist thing:

> ... dans cette loi des retraites ouvrières ... est tout le problème politique et sociale ... travaillons tous ensemble à améliorer, dans la manière si faible où peut le loi, le sort des individus; faisons-le; mais n'oublions jamais que le rôle de l'Etat n'est point de faire à chaque individu sa vie propre.[57]

The aim of the opposition was to obtain modifications in the bill which would weaken it. The government helped to do this when, in a letter to the Senate committee in 1908, it announced that the annual contribution of the state to the pension fund must be less than a third of the sum estimated to service the scheme under consideration. Although the government relaxed its conditions when Cuvinot (Gauche radicale), a fairly conservative member of the Centre, reported the modified bill to the Senate at the end of 1909 he felt bound to defend it at great length against the charge that it was inadequate.[58]

Some of the Right thought that this was the moment for a tactical retreat. Ribot announced his adherence (with reservations) to the obligatory principle which he, in common with the rest of the Right, had

---

[56] *J.O.*, February 23, 1906, pp. 975–6.
[57] *Conférence de M. Jules Roche ... et de M. Paul Beauregard au cirque de Rouen, le 1er avril 1906* (Rouen, 1906), p. 28.
[58] *J.O. Sénat*, November 5, 1909.

ing the tax in 1896, the year Paul Doumer introduced a bill to the

combated. The principle, he said, had become more generally acceptable to public opinion, and the Belgian compulsory scheme, which had been in operation since 1900, had worked well.[59] One of the leading Catholic senators, Raoul Ancel (Dr.), also accepted the Committee's bill. There was still plenty of vocal opposition to the measure. The Progressistes Audiffred and Touron and the monarchists Dominique Delahaye, Lamarzelle and Montfort made fundamental criticisms of it. The main points they raised were that the bill would not work because the majority of the country was against it; private pension schemes in conjunction with the Caisse Nationale des Retraites (which had been in operation since 1850) were providing adequate service; it would be difficult to invest the large sums necessary for a funded scheme with reasonable security (or, alternatively, that the government would appropriate the fund in times of need); the scheme would encourage rather than arrest the growth of socialism.

Few politicians cared to take their opposition to pensions through to the bitter end. Only five had voted against the bill in the Chamber in 1906, only three voted against the modified bill in the Senate on March 22, 1910 and only three in the Chamber on March 30 1910. After it was passed the most serious criticisms of the scheme came from the Socialists who considered it inadequate. But there continued to be criticism from the Right. In May 1911 a Radical senator, Codet, joined a monarchist, Brager de La Ville-Moysan, in interpellating the government on the *règlement administratif* of the pensions law. The government, however, was proceeding so cautiously that there was nothing for a conservative opposition to get its teeth into.

The older moderate Republicans had a long record of active opposition to income tax. Jules Roche (R.P.) was *rapporteur* in 1888 for the first bill to be examined by the Chamber. He published a book attacking the tax in 1896, the year Paul Doumer introduced a bill to the Chamber. No member of the Right had campaigned actively in favour of the tax and inevitably the Right was hostile to the bill Caillaux proposed on February 7, 1907. The bill was welcomed by an immediate drop in the value of government securities and some industrial equities. Edouard Aynard (R.P.) and Joseph Massabuau (A.L.) thought that this proved the iniquity of the measure.[60] Jules Roche wrote a series of ten articles in *la République française* during February and March 1907 attacking the bill from all angles. In three articles he was at pains to

[59] *J.O. Sénat*, November 9, 1909, especially p. 877.
[60] *J.O.*, February 8, 1907, pp. 342–5.

prove that the bill was opposed to the theory and practice of the great Revolution. Other newspapers of the Right joined in the campaign.

Roche, who made twenty-five major interventions during the debate of the Caillaux bill, argued that there was much wrong with the existing system of taxation but that the proposed reform was impractical, because of difficulties of assessment, and wrong in principle. Progressivity was the essential feature of the bill and progressive taxation "porte atteinte au principe de l'égalité". It would further the cause of socialism and would become:

> . . . un instrument de guerre sociale et de destruction économique . . . et c'est pour cela que ceux qui veulent renverser la société actuelle par la suppression de la propriété et du capital, veulent se servir de cet instrument.[61]

He rejected the analogies with other countries, saying that the problems of France were peculiar. He alleged that the tax would adversely affect the expansion and the adaptability of the economy.

Most of the other vocal members of the Right repeated Roche's arguments. The most popular argument was that income tax was opposed to the French character; favouritism and abuses were regarded by the Right as inevitable in Latin countries.[62] Alexandre Ribot (R.P.) defended the existing system of "quatre contributions directes" on the grounds that they provided a solid base for the budget and they required minimum contact between the tax collector and the citizen. Liberals, such as Jacques Piou and Louis Ollivier, favoured a cautious reform of the existing system and thus implied that they preferred it to the proposed income tax. The extreme Right tried to spread alarm rather than present a reasoned criticism of the bill. The marquis de Rosanbo (Ind.) argued that "sous un luerre de dégrèvements nous marchons à une augmentation des impôts". The marquis de Dion thought that the increase would be used "à augmenter la quantité des fonctionnaires dont un grand nombre ne travaille qu'à empêcher les autres de travailler".[63] Only the abbé démocrate, Jules Lemire, supported the bill:

> . . . parce qu'il renferme le principe de l'impôt personnel et global sur le revenu (Applaudissements à gauche et à l'extrême gauche);

[61] J.O., February 7, 1908, p. 257.
[62] E.g., Edouard Aynard, J.O., February 17, 1908, p. 351.
[63] J.O., February 12, 1908, pp. 310–13; February 17, 1908, p. 356.

ensuite parce qu'il renferme le principe de l'impôt progressif (Applau dissements sur les mêmes bancs – interruptions à droite). [64]

There were, however, variations in the seriousness with which members of the Right opposed income tax. Only fifty-six of the Right voted against discussing the articles of the Caillaux bill. Most of the Liberals voted in favour of discussion. By doing this they thought that they might obtain concessions.

There were certain sections of the Caillaux proposal which aroused the particular ire of the Right. The important principle of taxing the *rente française* was one of these. On this the Right gained a little support from the Centre. A Radical, Aimond, joined the Progressistes, Bouctot, Ribot and Roche, in condemning the proposal as a breach of the undertaking made in the law of 9 vendémaire an VI, and repeated by all subsequent governments, not to tax interest on Government loans.[65] All asserted that this breach of faith and the decline of real income derived from government loans would damage the credit of the state. Over thirty members of the Centre joined the Right in voting against the tax. Surprisingly, twenty-five of the Right voted for it.[66]

The Right was particularly sensitive to the taxation of agriculture. During the discussion of article three of the income tax bill, the vicomte de Villebois-Mareuil (Ind.) suggested that agricultural profits should be exempt from the tax because they were impossible to assess and because impositions on agriculture were already too heavy.[67] His amendment to article three was supported by all the important men of the extreme Right and the article survived in its original form by only thirty votes.[68] This was the closest that a major amendment proposed by the extreme Right came to success during the period 1905 to 1919.

[64] *J.O.*, February 17, 1908, p. 357.

[65] Roche, *J.O.*, May 21, 1908, pp. 1012–19; Aimond, May 22, 1908, pp. 1025–33; Ribot, May 25, 1908, pp. 1048–56; Bouctot, May 25, 1908, pp. 1057–1058.

[66] These were not monarchists hoping that the tax would damage the credit of the Republic but nineteen Progressistes, three Liberals and three Independents of *tendance gauche*.

[67] *J.O.*, March 9, 1909, p. 535.

[68] 271 votes to 240. After *rectifications de vote* this majority was reversed (by deputies who were looking over their shoulder to the agricultural interest in their constituencies but who did not want to associate with an attack led by the extreme Right in the Chamber). The government and committee introduced a very complicated compromise proposal which was passed by the Chamber on October 20, 1909.

Tax exemptions for the poor aroused strong feelings and had obvious electoral significance. The abbé Lemire (Ind.) proposed an extension to exemption from the tax in an amendment to article 15. His amendment was vigorously supported by the two extremes of the Chamber but was defeated by 299 votes to 235 on February 17, 1909. There were other amendments proposed from the Right with the object of securing further exemption but none collected so many votes.

The Chamber voted the bill on March 9, 1909 (nineteen members of the Right voted for it) and the Senate immediately elected a committee hostile to the bill. The Senate was so slow in discussing the measure that in 1914 Caillaux, once again Minister of Finance, decided to force its hand. He introduced a bill to impose a progressive capital tax and to start liquidating the old *contributions directes*. A motion proposed by a Radical senator, Perchot, which was voted by 140 votes to 134, destroyed the bill.[69] Soon afterwards the Senate rejected the principle of taxing the *rente française* by a similar majority. The writing was on the wall; the Senate could not resist the will of the Chamber on a money bill with such a small majority.

Caillaux tried to write income tax into the budget but the relevant articles were not discussed before the elections of 1914. An increased number of deputies were elected who were committed to the tax and the younger deputies of the Right were preparing to accept it. For example, Rochereau a newly elected Liberal deputy for Vendée, said immediately after the election that he could see nothing wrong with the tax in principle.[70] It was Ribot who broke the back of the opposition in the Senate to income tax. When he formed his ministry just after the elections he felt compelled to give an assurance that he would press the Senate to pass the income tax bill in order to attract votes from the Left. He did not succeed and his ministry was defeated on its first appearance before the Chamber. But, as a result of this undertaking, Ribot dropped his opposition to income tax. When, at the beginning of July 1914, Boivin-Champeux (Gauche radicale) and Lamarzelle (Dr.) proposed the *disjonction* of the article of the budget containing the principle of the income tax, Ribot opposed them. The motion was defeated by 207 votes to 70. A more subtle amendment by the Progressiste Touron was defeated by a similar majority. The opposition was now reduced exclusively to senators of the Right who did not, however, carry their opposition to the length of voting against the budget.

[69] February 25, 1914. All the senators of the Right voted with the majority.
[70] *La Gazette de France*, June 9, 1914.

The tax went into operation at the end of 1915 although an income tax bill was not passed until July 1917. In the final divisions only one deputy, Jules Roche, and no senator voted against it.

The passing of the three measures – nationalization of the Western Railway, old age pensions and income tax – quickly removed them from political debate. The nationalization question could not last long as a major political issue. No obvious injustice had been done. The shareholders of the company complained little about the transaction. The newspapers of the Right began to give prominence to accidents and inefficiencies on the Western Railway. Jules Roche and his Ligue pour la Défense des Contribuables continued to attack the nationalization of the Western Railway until the first world war. In 1914 the congress of Action Libérale called for a sharp reduction in its running costs. But this was about all that was done to keep the issue alive. The change in control of the railway – and it was this that the Right feared most – probably affected adversely the influence of the "social powers" in the West. But it did so imperceptibly.

The pensions bill passed by the Chamber in 1906 was not a drastic measure and the law eventually passed was even more modest. But it was the first law passed in France which brought about a small but general redistribution of income. It was a difficult measure for the Right to oppose as it was intended to help the poor and less fortunate members of the community. The Right traditionally felt that this was the duty of private individuals and not of the State but socially conscious members of the Right such as Albert de Mun (A.L.) had long been preaching that private initiative was not enough. Opposition to the pensions bill was therefore hesitant and uncertain. After it was passed the only effective pressure, even in the constituencies of the Right, was towards increasing the pensions rather than abolishing them. In the year preceding the election of 1919 the only comments made by parliamentarians of the Right on pensions were in favour of increasing them.

After the end of the war there was no movement among parliamentarians for the repeal of the income tax bill. There were remarkably few attacks on it in the press. An occasional polemic resurrected the spirit of pre-war controversial writing,[71] and le Temps attacked the tax during the election campaign of 1919.[72] The Right had more immediate measures to urge than the repeal or reform of the income tax law.

[71] E.g. l'Echo de Paris, July 26, 1919.
[72] Le Temps, October 23, 1919.

It was concerned to dismantle the apparatus which had been built up during the war to control the economy. Denys Cochin (Dr.) wrote:

> L'étatisme, qui a bien servi pendant la guerre, n'a pas laissé les bons souvenirs. On est las des consortiums, des taxations, des interventions perpétuelles de l'état. . . . On a soif d'initiative commerciale.[73]

There were some financial measures enforced during the war which the Right found more objectionable than income tax. The moratorium on rents and the excess profits tax (with some reservations) were the two most important.

Moreover the political implications of repeal agitation could have been undesirable. Maurice Barrès (Ind.) noted in his *Cahiers*:

> On a combattu l'impôt sur le revenu. Est-il question de revenir la-dessous?
>
> Les lois ne peuvent pas être rejetées maintenant, et la seule an- nonce qu'on voudrait les remettre en question déterminerait une poussée d'anticléricalisme funeste pour les catholiques.[74]

Apart from these practical considerations the arguments which the Right had used against income tax were being undermined. The tax had worked and there had been no political discrimination in assess- ment. When the elections of 1919 produced a majority which the Right approved, the latter consideration became irrelevant. This majority confirmed the tax by voting an important increase in it.[75]

There was between 1905 and 1919 an important shift in right wing opinion on the principles of progressive taxation and redistribution of wealth. In 1905 a majority of the Centre accepted with reluctance a limited application of these principles and the Right (with a few ex- ceptions) opposed them. Members of the extreme Right opposed them on political rather than economic grounds – they were not enamoured of laissez-faire principles. It was clear that such opposition could not persist long after the measures were passed. Progressiste opposition was based on economic principles. But for them continued opposition to the measures would have exacted too heavy a political price.

But the dividing line between Right and Centre on the issues of

---

[73] D. Cochin, *1914–1922*, Vol. I (1923), p. 173.
[74] M. Barrès, *Mes Cahiers*, Vol. XII (1957), p. 193.
[75] *J.O.*, April 29, 1920. The majority in favour of the increase was 499 to 72. The extreme Left formed the opposition. An ex-Progressite, Raiberti, was *rapporteur* for the measure.

"welfare economics" was always less clear than on the clerical issue. The Centre was concerned primarily with placing obstacles in the path of socialism. The Right at least had sympathy with this motive even if it disapproved of the tactics employed. Also the principles became submerged in the discussion of the detail of the measures. Their practical effects rather than the philosophy behind them became the predominant consideration for all deputies concerned with their constituents' interests.

Differences about the principles of welfare economics were as great and as deeply felt in 1919 as in 1905. But root and branch opposition to any application of these principles became a less reasonable position after the three measures – income tax, pensions and nationalization of the Western railway – had been applied. Reasonable conservatives like Ribot shifted their ground. Although members of the Right made disparaging remarks about the measures they did not campaign for their repeal. Like members of the Centre they became concerned to prevent further encroachments on the rights of property.

V

This legislation and the effects of the social disturbance of the years 1905 to 1911 blurred the differences between Right and Centre on the social question. This affected political alignments both inside and outside the Chamber. The attitudes of members of the Right towards governments changed.

During the period 1899 to 1914 members of the Right liked to refer to themselves as the "opposition". The term was convenient and it was accurate in that the most obvious attitude they had in common was opposition to the ministries of these years. But the concept of the Right as being by definition an opposition needs careful qualification even for the fifteen years preceding 1914.

Occasionally, representatives, and even a majority, of every group of the Right voted for motions of confidence, or of implied confidence, in governments. No section of the Right consistently opposed measures because they were backed by the government, although certain monarchists tended to do this. But voting for government supported legislation, and even giving a government general support over a period of time to facilitate the passage of a particular measure, did not mean that deputies regarded themselves or were regarded by others as part of the ministerial majority. This recognition came when groups consistently supported a government and were rewarded by representation in the cabinet. Neither support of nor opposition to particular pieces of legislation implied a corresponding attitude towards governments. This division was not peculiar to the French parliament but it was particularly clear there. Legislation was prepared for presentation to parliament, not by a minister, but by the appropriate committee of the Chamber or the Senate. Repeated rejection by the Chamber of articles of a bill which a government favoured could gravely weaken the prestige of the government. In order to get measures through parliament governments often had to make parts of them matters of confidence. This irritated the Right, especially the Progressistes.[76]

The government and the committees, all representing the majority of the Chamber, naturally held fairly similar views on legislation. Most of the conflicts were between governments and the relatively conservative Senate. But differences of opinion occurred between the Chamber committees and the government, partly because the leading members of the most important committees were contenders for ministerial office and partly because there were different majorities in the Chamber for different things. There was in the legislature 1910–14 a majority in the Chamber for electoral reform, but most government supporters were opposed to it. The president of the committee for electoral reform was the Progressiste, Charles Benoist and his most powerful supporter on the committee was Jaurès.

The attitude of the Right to governments was related to but separate from its attitudes to legislation. In the first place the discussion of important measures was frequently not completed within the span of one ministry; the debate on the Caillaux bill outlived nine ministries. Secondly, the Right favoured a prime minister who represented himself as a leader of the nation (although his ministry and declared policy conceded little to the Right) rather than a Republican who sought the support of Republicans only. Thirdly, the groups of the Right had particular views on their own nature and function which formed a background to their attitudes towards ministries. It was difficult for the monarchists to support ministers who thought that the existing constitution was the basis of social progress. Members of Action Libérale hoped that their group would one day be a great conservative party. As long as this hope lasted, continuous, though responsible, opposition was

[76] See the complaint of Jules Roche, *la République française*, November 16, 1909.

the order of the day. When it faded some Liberals tried to open the way to future co-operation with ministerial Republicans. Two distinct opinions gradually became apparent among Progressistes on the most desirable basis of a government. The conservative wing, led by Jules Roche, pinned their hopes on the electoral victory of the "opposition". They would provide the key members of any government which emerged from such a victory. On the other hand the aim of Joseph Thierry and his colleagues was to exclude the Socialists and the extreme Radical Socialists from the ministerial majority but include the Progressistes, thus moving the centre of gravity to the right. Thierry eventually insinuated himself into the ministerial majority but had to compromise so much that the majority of the Progressistes refused to follow him. In parliamentary terms, the main reason why a united conservative opposition, which seemed to be forming during the Combes and Rouvier administrations, was never realized was this division within the Progressiste group. Progressiste tactics had considerable practical importance for another reason; Progressiste votes sometimes helped to prolong the life of governments – the votes of the rest of the Right only served to bring them down.

All these factors influenced the attitudes of the Right to ministries during the period 1905–14. But the major consideration of members of the Right when they decided not to oppose, or to support, ministries was how much they thought the continued life of a ministry necessary for the preservation of the social status quo.

Occasionally a majority of Progressistes thought that the continuance of the Clemenceau administration was necessary. There was little in Clemenceau's personality or declared policy or composition of his ministry to appeal to the Right. His career evoked only painful memories and he was not conciliatory towards opponents. His cabinet, out of a total of eleven parliamentary ministers, contained five Radical Socialists and two independent Socialists. His declaration of policy was the most radical of the Third Republic until that of the Popular Front government of 1936. Yet twenty-seven Progressistes voted for the cabinet when it first appeared before the Chamber (October 25, 1906). Although the Progressistes never saved the government on a vote of confidence, they saved it from defeat on half a dozen other notable occasions. The cabinet could not possibly have lasted three years without intermittent Progressiste support. Those who voted for him at the beginning of his ministry were following a hallowed Progressiste tradition of not voting against a ministry until it did something deplorable. On subsequent occasions, as Albert de Mun explained,[77] they voted for him as a "man of order". When he took strong measures against strikers (and refused to take strong action against the Catholic resisters to the law of Separation) some Progressistes openly approved of his policy. But the compliments paid to his person were barbed: "Cet homme n'est peut-être admirable, mais il est imprévu. Il n'a pas les mêmes formules que les autres." But he could not satisfy them completely. Too frequently there was a coincidence of views between Clemenceau and the Socialists, which provoked outbursts of passionate indignation:

> Tout gouvernement qui laisse ébranler la confiance des citoyens dans la République en pactisant avec les révolutionnaires travaillent pour la réaction.
> Faites front à gauche. Tout le péril est là.[78]

There were elements in the majority which would have welcomed an understanding with the Progressistes and the formation of an anti-socialist ministry. Lamessan, Radical minister of Marine in the Waldeck-Rousseau cabinet, proposed in 1906 an alliance between the Radicals and the Progressistes for the purpose of mutual preservation against the Socialists and the reactionaries. He thought that the alliance between Progressistes and the rest of the Right was unnatural and that the Radicals were tired of serving the interests of the Socialists.[79] The Progressistes refused to take the proffered hand because, they argued, they would be compelled to adopt the social programme of the Radicals. Moreover, the behaviour of the Radicals since 1899, which Jules Roche stigmatized as "cette abominable politique qui est le contraire de la République",[80] had raised a barrier of ill-will which made any association with them impossible.

Louis Brindeau tried to define the official position of the Groupe Républicain Progressiste in his inaugural speech as president of the group in 1908. There were differences of opinion within the group concerning parliamentary tactics, but, he believed, the independent position of the group should be preserved. He described its position as that of an arbitrator. This was wishful thinking: there were not enough Progressistes to hold the government to ransom. Brindeau said that the

[77] Albert de Mun, *Combats d'hier et d'aujourd'hui*, Vol. II (1911), p. 11.
[78] *La République française*, February 5, 1907; October 1, 1908.
[79] *Le Siècle*, July 27, 1906; August 9 and 14, 1907.
[80] *La République française*, August 10, 1907.

group should support useful legislation and necessary policies but oppose harmful and offensive measures.[81] Most Progressistes desired, at this time, to give occasional support to the government but not general support, for the reasons which were expressed during the controversy over Lamessan's proposal.

The good will of Progressistes towards Clemenceau was extremely limited. They, like the extreme Right,[82] accused him of adopting their principles and abandoning his own whenever they approved of anything he did. The political temperature dropped immediately after his fall. Although Briand was Clemenceau's nominee, the personal contrast between the two men gave the impression of a great change.[83] Clemenceau was authoritarian and domineering and had ingrained, often-expressed Radical, Republican and anticlerical convictions. In contrast Briand seemed to change his opinions both as his personal role and the political climate shifted. Members of the Right hoped that he might evolve in a way favourable to them. This hope was encouraged by the respect with which he treated their convictions. Briand's personal magnetism also had a great effect.[84]

Briand's declaration of policy (July 27, 1909) committed his government to very little. On electoral reform, to which the Right was attaching ever greater significance, Briand was conciliatory. The reference to income tax was brief and non-commital; it was construed as the *de facto* abandonment of the Caillaux bill. Progressiste reactions were favourable. In the first months of the ministry there was usually a majority of the Progressiste group which was prepared to vote confidence in the government. It was not long before the ultra-catholic

[81] *La République française*, April 1, 1908. Brindeau repeated the substance of this statement in the Chamber a few days later and Clemenceau made a conciliatory reply. *J.O.* April 6, 1908, pp. 889–94.

[82] See the attacks of Delahaye (Ind.) and Bougère (Ind.) *J.O.*, June 28, 1907, p. 592.

[83] Not only was Briand Clemenceau's nominee but ten out of the fourteen ministers in the new administration had held office under Clemenceau. The most important change was the replacement of Caillaux by Cochery (Union démocratique) at the Ministry of Finance. Barthou's promotion from Public Works to Justice added further weight to the moderate element of the cabinet. The total Radical Socialist representation in the cabinet declined from seven to three.

[84] Denys Cochin (Ind.) averred in a private letter (to Mme Pierre d'Harcourt, July 1909, Cochin MSS.) that he had "un faible pour Briand". Renaud d'Elissagary (R.N.) by temperament a violent oppositionist described how he was swayed by admiration for Briand. R. d'Elissagary, *Mémoires* (MS.), pp. 136–137. There had been Progressiste admirers of Briand for some time.

Rocafort was complaining in *l'Univers* that the Progressistes were coming to form a permanent part of the ministerial majority.[85] Rocafort added that the Liberals were not making "liberty" the first of their considerations. A majority of Action Libérale had abstained and four of them, the most prominent being Joseph Massabuau, had voted confidence in Briand. Massabuau explained why:

> Nous ne voulons pas voir élever entre la République et nous le barrière du dogme laïque: et cela au profit de petits comités qui sous couleur de l'anticléricalisme veulent nous dominer.[86]

They did not want the religious question to prevent them supporting a ministry with which they were in general agreement. This had been the Progressiste position since the passing of the law of Separation. In the Lamessan controversy Progressistes had only incidentally raised the religious issue although Lamessan bore personal responsibility for the passing of the anticlerical measures affecting the navy. Massabuau was attacked from the extreme Right by Jules Delahaye (Ind.) who said that he had not even tried to get concessions on religious policy.[87] Delahaye and others thought that it was not enough that a government should be sound on social policy. They suspected that some of the Liberals had made a bargain with Briand over the forthcoming general elections.

It is unlikely that there was such a bargain and in any case there were more general reasons for Massabuau's behaviour. There was a sense in which the Briand ministry was one of *détente à droite*. In his most famous statement, the speech at Périgueux in October 1909, Briand called for the liquidation of political tension, an end to division and strife in the country and a "Republic open to all". Making no concessions to the Left, he was evasive about income tax, hinted at the possibility of electoral reform and made a rousing appeal to patriotic sentiment. Progressiste reactions to the speech were wholly favourable. Briand had echoed recurrent themes in the speeches of Progressiste leaders. Important Progressistes and Liberals, Beauregard and Roche, Piou and de Mun, preserved the posture of opposition but they seemed unwilling to press their criticisms. Briand disconcerted the Right. During the election campaign of 1910 the newspapers of the Right were full of discussions of Briand and his policy of *apaisement*. Most of the Right were not sure whether Briand was sincere or whether he could put his policy

---

[85] *L'Univers*, November 6, 1909.   [86] *J.O.*, January 19, 1910, p. 203.
[87] *L'Autorité*, January 20, 1910.

into practice. They seemed to think that Briand was hinting at a policy which they desired but at the same time they feared that Briand was cutting the ground from under their feet. If Briand was forced to rely on the votes of the Right this would have been excellent but if he succeeded in posing as the man of order, of social and religious peace with a policy of go-slow on social and financial reforms whilst, at the same time, succeeding in basing his ministry on a Radical and Centrist majority, even more of the electorate might think that the continued existence of the Right was pointless. And Briand showed no inclination to govern with a majority which included the Right.

The highwater mark of Briand's popularity in the Right as a whole was in October 1910 when he defended the breaking of a railway strike by saying that he would use illegal methods if necessary to defend the essential services of the community. Whilst the Socialists heckled Briand, the Right stood up as one man and cheered him to the echo.[88] This display of enthusiasm for a prime minister was unique in the fifteen years preceding 1914. The reasons were twofold: the Right had every sympathy for determined measures against working class agitation; and the authoritarian tone of Briand's statement appealed to the authoritarian temperament of the Right, echoing the aphorism of Louis Napoleon: "Nous sortirons de la légalité pour rentrer dans le droit." In the vote Briand depended upon the support of the Right: only three of its members, Baudry d'Asson, Delahaye and Lavrignais, voted against the government in accordance with the *politique du pire*.

Shortly afterwards, in order to avoid the accusation of collusion with the Right, Briand reconstructed his cabinet and included Lafferre, sometime master of the Grand Orient and defender of the system of *fiches de délation* operated during the Combes ministry. The Right interpreted this as a slap in the face. Denys Cochin (Dr.) wrote in a private letter:

> Briand n'invite pas la Droite à son banquet. C'est entendu. . . .
> Mais il fait plus. Il fait comme le vieux Guillaume I de Prusse qui . . .
> voulant empêcher ses enfants de dîner avec lui crachait dans les
> plats. C'est ce qu'a fait Briand en nous offrant Lafferre.[89]

The Right did not swing unanimously into opposition. Joseph Massabuau (A.L.) and Edouard Aynard (R.P.) who had both spoken in

[88] Information given to the author in February 1960 by the late Adrien Thierry who was present at the sitting.
[89] Letter to Mme Pierre d'Harcourt, November 22, 1911, Cochin MSS.

support of Briand after the elections of 1910 did not comment on the new cabinet. Paul Beauregard (R.P.) said he would vote for the cabinet because of the assurances given in the ministerial declaration for the "defence of society".[90] The Progressiste group split: those favouring co-operation with Briand re-formed the Union Républicain under the presidency of Joseph Thierry. In doing this they so denied their past that they cannot, from this time, be regarded as members of the Right. They were adopting the same position as Poincaré, Jonnart, Barthou and other members of the Centre who disapproved of *combisme* but condoned it.

Briand managed to exert an attraction still further to the Right. Maurice-Binder (Ind.) restated a doctrine which had been expressed with greater *éclat* by Clemenceau five years previously. There were, he said, only two parties in 1910, the party of order and the party of revolution: both Briand and himself belonged to the former so he would vote for the cabinet in spite of Lafferre.[91] But there were still Progressistes, Liberals, Nationalists and monarchists who denounced Briand and Lafferre in accents which recalled the struggles of former days.

Briand's "anti-radicalism", and his revival of the ideas of *concentration républicaine* and *esprit nouveau* used by Méline and Spuller in the nineties,[92] were potentially of great parliamentary significance. A ministry of the Centre supported by Republicans of the Right was once again within the bounds of possibility. Briand's ministry never approached this condition. When he said "je ne veux exclure personne de ma majorité", he also made it quite clear that he required the support of the Left. When at the end of his second ministry, he came to rely on the votes of the Right on religious policy, he resigned.

All the ministries from 1911 to 1914 were influenced by the experience of Briand's first period in power: they either revived the ideas of *apaisement* and national unity or, conversely manifested a belief in the desirability of party strife. The threat from Germany and the alleged necessity to extend the period of military service from two to three years made respectable Rightist support for ministries who declared that their first aim was the defence of the interests and the prestige of the country. The alternative combinations (those of Poincaré, Briand,

[90] *J.O.*, November 9, 1910. pp. 2712–15. In spite of this statement Beauregard did not join the Thierry split.

[91] *J.O.*, November 9, 1910, p. 2727.

[92] See particularly Briand's declaration *J.O.*, June 9, 1910, pp. 2082–4. Characteristically he used a great many more words than Spuller.

Barthou as against Monis, Caillaux and Doumergue) did not present radically different cabinets. The same men often held the key posts in both combinations. The tone of the cabinets was set by outstanding men such as Caillaux, Malvy, Briand and Poincaré who held controversial and widely known views on general policy.

The short-lived ministry of Monis (who replaced Briand), despite the moderation of the leading ministers and a declaration about income tax which was even more equivocal than Briand's aroused the violent hostility of the Right. Even a républicain de gauche, Léon Bérard, accused the government of being associated with revolutionary socialism, although the Socialists did not vote for the government. The reason for this hostility was the inclusion of Caillaux in the cabinet as Minister of Finance. The Right reacted against the ideas of Caillaux for much the same reasons that it favoured some of Briand's. Caillaux claimed that the Radical party was "l'expression même de la démocratie française" and the attempt to realize "l'union de tous les français" was chimerical, dangerous and reactionary. The struggle between the party of progress and the party of reaction was still, as it had been since the foundation of the Republic, the major issue in politics.[93] Such ideas implied the revival of the *bloc des gauches* and of old quarrels. Though no revival of the *bloc* took place – the Socialists voted against the investiture of Caillaux as prime minister on June 30, 1911 – the threat alarmed the Right. It made a huge outcry about the antipatriotic nature of the Caillaux cabinet after the Moroccan crisis of 1911. In doing so it committed itself in spirit to support his successor, Raymond Poincaré.

Having built up the German threat as the most important political issue, members of the Right were bound, unless they indulged in rapid intellectual contortions, to vote for Poincaré who was nominated because he was known to differ from Caillaux on foreign policy. After receiving an impressive vote of confidence on January 16, 1912, Poincaré succeeded in retaining, without making any concrete concessions, the goodwill of the Right for a year, at the end of which it supported his candidature for the presidency of the Republic. He started with certain advantages as far as the Right was concerned. He had a *revanchard* past and (partly because he came from Lorraine) was regarded as the epitome of patriotism. His reputation and record as a careful, conservative financier, gave him admirers, if not partisans on the Right. He gave the impression that he was not soiled by the system. His almost

[93] See his Saint-Calais speech: *Le Temps*, November 6, 1911.

complete abstention from politics during the Dreyfus Affair and the Separation crisis helped him. But, although out of sympathy with sectarian anticlericalism, he regarded the lay laws as sacred. He was not prepared to associate in public with anyone tainted with clericalism.

His declaration of policy struck the right note. The duty of his government, he said, was to group all sections of the "Republican party" under the banner of national sentiment:

> Pour réaliser cette union, nous n'avons qu'à suivre l'exemple du pays qui, toujours indifférent aux questions de personnes, doit, aux heures difficiles, s'élever sans peine à la claire compréhension de l'intérêt public.[94]

This was an appeal, popular on the Right, to the *pays réel*. Poincaré promised strong government and close attention to national defence; domestic policy appeared of secondary importance. Only defence of the *école laïque* provoked a protest from the Right. Millevoye (Ind.) said that Nationalists would support Poincaré as long as he governed in the spirit of his declaration.[95] Albert de Mun in *l'Echo de Paris* (January 20, February 24, March 11 and 18, 1912) extolled the "noble language" of Poincaré.

The key to Poincaré's success in retaining the "réserve sympathique"[96] of the Right lay in his clever handling of the electoral reform issue, in his reticence on the subject of income tax and in his statements on foreign policy. Suggestions that France should be ready for war and that Russia could rely on France if she was forced to go to war in the Balkans appealed to Nationalist and militarist sentiments. Moreover, the organizations of the Right were in decay. Deep pessimism was expressed at their congresses. At the moment when nationalist ideas were gaining wider adherence the only party which had sent deputies to the Palais Bourbon – the Ligue de la Patrie française, went out of existence. Lacking organizations and an outstanding leader the Right looked outside its own ranks for a national leader. There was nothing peculiar about this. It is a recurrent phenomenon in the history of French democracy.

[94] *J.O.*, January 16, 1912, p. 11.

[95] *Ibid.*, pp. 14–15.

[96] Phrase used by Piou to define his own attitude towards Poincaré. J. Piou, *D'une guerre à l'autre* (1932) p. 262. According to Piou, de Mun was the leader of the pro-Poincaré sentiment on the Right and two letters written by de Mun during the period of the presidential election show his close identification with Poincaré's cause. F. Payen, *Raymond Poincaré* (1936), pp. 389–92.

But the social question subsumed all these considerations. The Right did not oppose Poincaré, and more particularly it did not oppose his successors Briand and Barthou,[97] ostensibly for patriotic reasons but really because it wanted to bar the way of Caillaux. Albert de Mun wrote to Denys Cochin in March 1913 (at the height of the campaign for the three years law) that it was necessary to avoid any "aventures présidentielles" and: "Il faut à tout prix éviter Caillaux, et tout ce qui divise les voix anti-radicales lui profite." [98] The manner in which the Right conducted the campaign for the three years bill suggested that the object was as much to intimidate its opponents and to create a barrier between "patriotic" and "socialistic" Radicals (in the hope of making a government of the Left impossible) as to pass the bill itself.[99] In spite of the anticlericalism of the Barthou government, which was necessary in order to ensure its majority, the Right did not withdraw support from the government once the three years bill was passed.

Le Temps (December 3, 1913) accused the Liberals of pursuing the politique du pire because Piou and de Mun assisted the downfall of Barthou by helping to elect a hostile rapporteur for the loan to meet the cost of the three years law. Piou indignantly denied the charge, saying that he thought that the money should be raised by increased taxation of the wealthy.[100] The charge was inconsistent with the attitude of de Mun and Piou to the Fédération des gauches, the new party founded by Barthou, Millerand and Briand in December 1913. De Mun (l' Echo de Paris, December 15, 1913) and Piou (l'Eclair, December 18, 1913) wrote offering their support. They were criticized by the extreme Right and Briand rejected their support to the indignation of de Mun. It is difficult to see why they acted in this way if they deliberately plotted the downfall of Barthou. Moreover, in the vote (December 2, 1913 on the immunity of the loan from taxation) which defeated Barthou the Right solidly supported the government.

Barthou was succeeded by the Radical Doumergue who said he desired support from the Left only and chose Caillaux as Minister of Finance. The Right was bitterly and unanimously hostile to his govern-

[97] The Right was less well-disposed to their ministries although Briand said he intended to carry on Poincaré's policy and Joseph Thierry (U.R.) was included in Barthou's cabinet. Both met with considerable Radical hostility but neither Briand nor Barthou was as acceptable to the Right on religious and personal grounds.

[98] Letter dated March 5, 1913; Cochin MSS.

[99] For this campaign see G. Michon, La Préparation à la guerre (1935), pp. 137 ff.

[100] J.O., November 28, 1913, p. 2662.

ment. After the elections of 1914 which returned an increased number of supporters for the three years law and electoral reform but a diminished number of opponents of income tax and the *lois laïques*, Poincaré charged Ribot (now a member of the Senate group, Gauche républicaine) to form a ministry. This was self-defence on the part of the president of the Republic – he wished to show his disillusioned admirers the impossibility of a moderate ministry. Ribot gave formal commitments to support income tax and *laïcité* but was rejected by the Chamber. Not one member of the Right either voted against him or abstained. Viviani succeeded him and presented much the same programme. He defended the three years law and this inhibited many of the Right. Eighty-five abstained when Viviani presented his ministry.

When war was declared and Poincaré pronounced the famous slogan of *union sacrée*, the Right renounced opposition and even the right to criticize governments. In private there was obviously a considerable amount of criticism.[101] But only once did a deputy of the Right come near to launching a general attack on the government. Ybarnégaray (Ind.) in the secret session of June 29, 1917 described the bloody and pointless offensive of April 1917 (he had played an important part behind the scenes in ending it) and accused those who had appointed Nivelle commander-in-chief of bearing a heavy responsibility.[102] Since Ybarnégaray was a partisan of Pétain all his attack eventually amounted to was that the government had done the right thing too late. The Right as a whole only once used its votes against a government during the war. This was on the occasion of Painlevé's defeat in November 1917. But Painlevé was also attacked from the Left and the Centre. On legislation and matters of domestic policy the Socialistes unifiés formed the opposition about six times more frequently than the Right. In spite of this self-abnegation only one member of the Right, Denys Cochin (Dr.) was given office during the war.[103]

[101] Emmanuel Brousse (Gauche démocratique) wrote to the ex-nationalist deputy, Renaud d'Elissagaray (June 6, 1916) that "On ne fait rien à la Chambre que comploter contre le cabinet" '– D'Elissagaray MSS. A diarist, Germain Bapst, who frequented the *salons* of the nationalist and extreme Right recorded criticisms of every government save Clemenceau's; G. Bapst, *Journal de la grande guerre*, 8 MS. vols.

[102] This speech made a considerable impression on the Chamber – letter of Georges Leygues to Renaud d'Elissagaray, July 5, 1917 – D'Elissagaray MSS.

[103] Cochin was influential in such matters as the blockade, relations with Rome and on legislative proposals such as the bill on war orphans. Three ex-members of the Right – Ribot, Lebrun and Thierry – held office during the war.

The behaviour of the Right was governed by two factors. Immediately before the war it had made a fetish of national unity. In wartime the practice of national unity meant standing firmly behind the government. Also, the way in which government was conducted approximated more closely to the ideas of the Right. Control of the conduct of the war by the legislature was difficult. Control of the government in public session of the Chamber was inappropriate and the committees were found ineffective for this purpose. The infrequent secret sittings of the Chamber were the only way. The demand for a secret session was regarded as an expression of lack of confidence in a government and the Right was reluctant to join in such demands. The share of the Chamber in policy-making was, therefore, much reduced. This reduction was one of the few aims of constitutional reform upon which all elements of the Right were agreed. When, in July 1917, a proposal was made to strengthen parliamentary control over the conduct of the war, Louis Marin (F.R.) and Jacques Piou (A.L.) combated it strongly.

During the war and afterwards until the elections of 1919 the Right behaved very much as government supporters had done before the war. Members of the Right were discreet in their remarks about the men in power; they showed their disapproval by withholding praise rather than by any positive act. It was difficult to tell exactly what they thought of many developments from their public statements. There were exceptional cases. The effusive praise received by Poincaré for calling upon Clemenceau to form a ministry was a certain indication that the Right approved. The Right, like ministerial deputies before the war, voted indiscriminately for successive governments. When the sectional interests of members of the Right were involved in a particular measure they were prepared to oppose it without extending their attack to a general one on the government. Finally, when further support of a government (as with the Painlevé cabinet) seemed likely to have disastrous consequences, they withdrew their support with dramatic suddenness.[104]

Although during the Poincaré and Barthou administrations in 1912 and 1913 the Right behaved in some of these ways, it was more like an opposition which had temporarily ceased to oppose. They were not

---

[104] There were some deputies who showed oppositionist tendencies throughout the war – notably Baudry d'Asson (Dr.) Lavrignais (Dr.) and the independents, Poirer de Narçay, Chappedelaine, Fougère and Lagrosillière. But Clemenceau satisfied even the malcontents.

accepted as regular government supporters. There was a real change of role by the Right in parliament during the exceptional circumstances of the war. It was recognized by others. Only once was a part of the Right reminded of its "anti-Republicanism" in parliament[105] and the clerical issue was played down as far as possible. The government required and desired the support of all sections of opinion, and those which supported it consistently were naturally looked on with favour. Thus members of the Right were rehabilitated and looked on once again as people with whom it was possible to co-operate.

The war, therefore, gave impetus to the evolution which had been set in motion by the social problem. The doctrine of *union sacrée* gave a tactical advantage to the Right over its *bêtes noires*, Caillaux, Malvy and the Socialists. In 1917 Caillaux and Malvy were arraigned for treasonous contacts with the enemy, and the Socialists, although Guesde, Thomas and Sembat had accepted office, grew more and more restive about the political truce. This gave the Right the opportunity to brand its enemies as unpatriotic. There is a parallel between the campaign in favour of the three years' law and the eagerness of the Right to continue the *union sacrée* into the peace. Although the spirit of the *union sacrée* was broken for the Right by the debate on the Peace treaties, this eagerness affected the alignment of the electoral parties for the elections of November 1919.

VI

The evolution of the Right in the Chamber from a condition of isolated opposition in 1905 to a partial and hesitant alignment behind Poincaré, Briand and Barthou in the period 1912 to 1914 was hardly reflected at all in the country. Some individuals changed their electoral tactics and others tried to change them. In 1910 Joseph Thierry forswore the *anti-blocard* polemics of the previous election and adopted the language of Briand. In 1914 his candidature in the third constituency of Marseilles was sponsored by the Centrist Alliance Démocratique (with which he had come to have much in common) as well as the Progressiste party, the Fédération républicaine. Local opinion did not see any change. The Radical newspaper, *le Petit provençal*, commented (April

[105] On January 18, 1918, the government was interpellated on a work sponsored by Action française, which mentioned the royalist sympathies of certain officers. Against the violent opposition of the extreme Right a motion was passed condemning Royalist and other plots against the Republic.

21, 1914): ". . . cette timide tentative d'évolution politique . . . laisse M. Thierry prisonnier de ses attaches réactionnaires locales." Although in 1910, the *bloc des gayches* was an artificial electoral combination and in 1914 it was little more than a slogan, most of the Right maintained the fiction that elections were fought on a national scale between the *bloc* on the one hand and all *anti-blocards* on the other. This was a useful fiction because the Right could pretend that it was defending France against "the Revolution" even when the particular opponent was a moderate member of the Centre. Naturally this kind of argument was more often used by and was more useful to the extreme Right. But at election times propagandists of the Right realized that the prerequisite of a united and combative Right was a united and militant Left. They tried to behave as if the latter existed; some probably believed it did.

In the three general elections of 1906, 1910 and 1914 formal electoral alliances on a national level between the parties of the Right and in the two later elections between elements of the Centre and the Right were scarcely possible because of traditional animosities and would, in any case, have been of little value to the participants. Even in 1906, when representatives of all sections of the Right from monarchists to Progressistes proclaimed the necessity of uniting the "opposition", no comprehensive electoral alliance was formed. The Liberals and Progressistes drew up a single list in Gironde, but this example did not inspire imitation in other departments. In 1910 and 1914 the adepts at electoral bargains and combinations, the right wing Radicals, the men of Alliance Démocratique and the Fédération des Gauches had little interest in making a deal with the Right because they were not seriously threatened from the Left. The return of over a hundred deputies at the election of 1914 was received by the newspapers of the Centre as a warning that it was necessary to make an effort on a national scale to halt the socialist advance. Even under normal conditions there would have been an attempt at the following election to assemble a comprehensive anti-socialist alliance.

The war produced considerable dislocation in the economy and in the everyday lives of most Frenchmen. The loss of so many able-bodied men was sufficient to cause a feeling of disorientation. The rapid expansion of certain sections of industry under the worst possible conditions during the war, the direction of labour and the necessarily painful readjustment to peacetime production after the war, exacerbated this feeling. On psychological grounds it seemed likely that more people would look to revolutionary change to alleviate physical hardships. The success of the Russian Revolution was an encouragement. The physical hardships were real and severe. The increase in the cost of living had affected all classes but it was felt more by industrial wage earners, civil servants and *rentiers* than by other sections of the community. Industrial disputes, which had not been unknown during the last eighteen months of the war became serious and bitter in 1919. In June, Paris and the important industrial regions of the provinces were affected by widespread and sometimes violent strikes of metal, chemical, transport and mine workers. These strikes and the extremist resolutions passed by the Socialist congress of April alarmed the bourgeoisie. The fear or the anticipation of revolution was much more apparent in 1919 than it had been at the height of the syndicalist agitation before the war. It was a time when all conservative men had the same major preoccupation. This was the main reason why the Right and the Centre were able to form an electoral coalition.

The vested political interests in the Right which might have put up a stout resistence to this coalition were in a weak condition in 1919. The electoral parties of the Right – the Fédération Républicaine, Action Libérale Populaire and the Ligue de la Patrie Française (which disappeared in 1912) – were decayed before 1914 and nothing during or immediately after the war revived them. Much more serious was the lack of leaders of any standing. Almost all the pre-war Progressiste leadership had left or was about to leave politics. Ribot was getting very old; Joseph Thierry and Aynard had died; Jules Roche, Benoist and Paul Beauregard were about to retire. The Liberal leadership was also melting away. De Mun died in 1914; Piou was about to retire; Gailhard-Bancel was getting old and L'Estourbeillon was too involved in Breton regionalism to be acceptable as a national leader. Of the younger men, Henri Bazire, who was considered as a possible successor to Piou and de Mun, had died as a result of gas poisoning; Joseph Denais was in bad odour with the ex-servicemens' organizations because of his unheroic war record. Jean Lerolle was the only experienced member of the so-called "équipe Bazire" who remained and he was defeated in the elections. On the extreme Right Millevoye, Berry and Delafosse had died. Denys Cochin was set on retirement. Lamarzelle was not prepared to hide his monarchist allegiance in order to gain a wider following. Maurice Barrès was respected and his views were widely applauded but as a leader and organizer he was of the second rank.

Lack of leaders and of serious organizations on the Right had several effects. The Right looked outside its own ranks for leadership. At this time the hero and father-figure of the Right was Clemenceau. Even those who opposed the Treaty of Versailles continued to pay hommage to his person. Although all the Right, including the monarchists, continued to honour him as a great national leader, and to support him as "le rempart national contre le bolchevisme",[106] Clemenceau had no desire to lead an electoral coalition in which the Right took part. Millerand tried to take his place. The crisis of leadership also meant that men such as Barrès and Marcel Habert (the old associate of Déroulède) suddenly achieved a prominence far beyond their talents. A score of would-be regenerators of France sprang up and formed a host of *ligues*. The names of the new groups generally reveal them as creatures of the nationalist euphoria of 1919 – Parti Républicain de Réorganization Nationale, Parti de Renouveau Français, IVᵉ République, Union Nationale Républicaine, Parti socialiste Français. It was not only on the extreme Left that there was hope for radical changes in politics.

The formation of a great anti-socialist coalition was a delicate matter. The first in the field to campaign for a coalition were the leaders of the Union Nationale Républicaine (founded in December 1918), Marcel Habert and Emile Massard. Both had long careers of violent nationalist agitation behind them and Centre Republicans therefore distrusted them. In the summer of 1919 it became obvious that most members of the Radical party would not co-operate with the Right. Briand also announced his public disapproval of the proposed alliance. Leadership of the projected "national" alliance devolved on a man of lesser reputation, Adolphe Carnot, president of the Parti Républicain Démocratique (formerly Alliance Démocratique). Carnot made overtures to the Radicals and was prepared to offend the Right on the clerical issue[107] but the Radicals rejected his offer. The Right then assumed greater importance to Carnot and his collaborators and concessions were made both by Carnot and by Millerand on religious policy. Both accepted and inserted in their programmes a compromise formula on *laïcité* drafted by Jacques Piou.[108] It is significant that the religious issue was the only issue which proved troublesome in the drawing up of the programme of the *Bloc national*. A thorough discussion of the problem took place between Barrès and Millerand during the formation of the

[106] Baudry d'Asson (Dr.), *J.O.*, August 29, 1919, p. 4160.
[107] See letter of Carnot to Edouard Herriot, president of the Radical party. *Le Temps*, September 28, 1919.
[108] Letter of Piou to Barrès, November 11, 1919. M. Barrès, *Mes Cahiers*, Vol. XII (1957), pp. 333–6.

national list in the second constituency of Paris. Denys Cochin (Dr.) found himself unable to support the *Bloc national* because he could not drop his opposition to the lay laws.[109] Some Catholics, particularly monarchists (who were excluded from the *bloc*) continued to complain after the election about the attitude of the *bloc* towards the laws, but there was no concerted opposition to the *bloc* on religious grounds.

There was no controversy at all on the social and financial sections of the programme of the *bloc*. These were vague and conservative: "liberté du travail, du commerce et de l'industrie"; the co-operation of intelligence, labour and capital to utilize national and colonial wealth to the best advantages; "Assainissement des finances publiques, lutte contre le gaspillage, équilibre sincère des budgets, limitation d'initiative parlementaire en matière de dépenses." Income tax was not mentioned and the proposed solution for the financial difficulties of France was to make Germany pay. The social reforms suggested were the extension of civil rights of professional associations, the setting up of arbitration tribunals for industrial disputes, undefined measures against tuberculosis, bad housing and demoralization, benefits for the family and the encouragement of the birth-rate, the development of social insurance and measures to assist the workers to acquire property. These doctrines had all figured in manifestos of parties of the Right before the war.

Freed from the necessity of respecting radical opinion the propagandists of the *bloc* became more and more conservative on financial and social questions. On October 23, 1919, *le Temps* (which acted almost as the official newspaper of the *bloc*) demanded the abolition of income tax and on October 28 condemned all the social reforms and wage increases currently demanded by the Socialists. None of the leaders of the *bloc* dared go as far as this. They avoided making specific commitments in order to preserve the appearance of unity.

By loudly asserting that the *bloc* was formed in order to preserve the *union sacrée* during the reconstruction and that patriotism was their only motive, the leaders of the coalition gained a moral and tactical advantage over their opponents. The central organization of the *bloc* was feeble and had no power over the composition of the lists in the constituencies throughout the country. It was a useful covering title for a variety of local combinations. There were three main types of combination: the first was the Millerand/Barrès type, the participants of which extended from dissident Radical Socialists to Nationalists and included the Liberals; the second extended from Radical Socialists to

[109] *Ibid.*, especially pp. 188–91, 322–8, 331–3. Also Cochin MSS.

Progressistes; the third comprised right of Centre Republicans and the Right (this was mainly restricted to the West). In those departments where the political situation was stable the electoral achievements before the war appeared to be the main basis for the composition of the lists. Their common features were that they excluded avowed monarchists (who were few) and were opposed by Socialists and the Radicals who did not wish to join an anti-socialist coalition. Their characteristics were a common platform of anti-socialism, and the inclusion of candidates to appeal to the traditional allegiances of the constituencies, interspersed with a considerable number of ex-servicemen and candidates new to national politics in order to satisfy a general desire for change.

The elections of November 1919 resulted in an overwhelming victory for the "national" lists – about 435 deputies were elected on these lists. The prominent politicians of the Centre handled a potentially awkward situation very successfully. The prime ministers accepted by the *Chambre bleu horizon* were all men who had had long and eminent ministerial careers before the war. The inexperience and general mediocrity of the new deputies of the Right elected in 1919 helped the old guard to preserve their hegemony. The new group, the Entente Républicaine Démocratique, founded under the presidency of François Arago to carry the apparent unity of the electoral arena into the Chamber did not succeed in asserting its claims to office and influence which its numbers warranted. It seemed that although the centre of gravity of the Chamber had moved to the Right nothing much had changed. There was an attempt to build up a mystique of the *Bloc national* but this was unsuccessful. Léon Daudet and other members of the extreme Right exacerbated the dormant divisions within it.

The long term effects of the formation of the *bloc* were slight. The moderate Republicans, split since 1899 into two factions (represented in the country by the Fédération Républicaine and Alliance Démocratique) came together again. They retained their separate identity but they co-operated. The religious issue was no longer important enough to divide them. But the Radicals, having completed their religious and social programmes, became in the inter-war period the most powerful defenders of the status quo. Most of them consistently rejected formal co-operation with Conservatives tainted with clericalism and they clung to the traditional position of having "no enemies on the Left". The clerical issue, traditional animosities, and the struggle for power and position lived on to divide conservative men.

© MALCOLM ANDERSON 1962

CHECK LIST OF PRINTED BIOGRAPHICAL MATERIAL ON PARLIAMENTARIANS OF THE THIRD REPUBLIC

Compiled by David Shapiro

THIS LIST is of works that furnish details supplementary to the notices of Robert, Bourloton and Cougny and of M. Jolly (see below, Section 1); it omits works of general French biography, such as those of Carnoy, Curinier, Prévost and Roman D'Amat, Vapereau, etc. It does not claim to be complete even for those works that contain biographies of all the members of a legislature, except in so far as they are catalogued in the Bibliothèque Nationale in *cote* Ln 6. For anonymous works untraceable in public catalogues the *cote* is given. (I have to thank the staff of the Bibliothèque Nationale for much assistance in the compilation of this section of the list.)

The fourth section is necessarily sketchy and is offered as a stimulus for others to improve upon. The finding list of "Barodets" is intended to provide a portable guide through the mass of *Documents parlementaires*, that of the *Notices et portraits* to indicate where they can be found.

All works published were published in Paris unless otherwise stated.

1. Biographies of parliamentarians of more than one legislature.
2. Biographies of the deputies of one legislature.
3. Biographies of the senators of one legislature.
4. Partial biographical surveys, including surveys by department, by economic interest or by party.
5. "Barodets".
6. *Notices et Portraits.*

1. Robert, A., Bourloton, E., and Cougny, G., *Dictionnaire des parlementaires français . . . depuis le 1er mai 1789 jusqu'au 1er mai 1889* (1889–91), 5 vols.

Jolly, J., *Dictionnaire des parlementaires français . . . de 1889 a 1940* (1960–). [In course of publication]

Samuel, R., and Bonet-Maury, G., *Les Parlementaires français. II. 1900–1914.* (1914). [Only this volume published]

The *Annuaire du Parlement* (1899–1913), edited from 1901 by R. Samuel and G. Bonet-Maury, contains biographical information under the varying rubrics "Travaux personnels", "Biographies parlementaires", "Nos parlementaires"

2. Bibeyre, F., *Biographie des représentants à l'Assemblée nationale* (Angers, n.d.)
— — second edition (Angers, 1872)

Clerc, A. V., *Nos députés à l'Assemblée nationale, leur biographie et leurs votes* . . . (October 1872)

Spoll, E. A., *Nos représentants et leurs votes* (1873)

[Duquesne, A.,]*Musée de l'Assemblée nationale contenant les portraits de tous les députés* (1874) [Portraits only]

Dutemple, E., *Guide impartial des électeurs, biographie et travaux des représentants à l'Assemblée nationale* (1874)

Clère, J., *Biographie des députés, avec leurs principaux votes depuis le 8 février 1871 jusqu'au 15 juin 1875* (1875)

— *Biographie complète des 533 députés par un sénateur* (1876) [B.N. Ln. 6. 109]

— *Biographie complète des cinq cent trente-quatre députés par trois journalistes* (1876) [Contains excerpts of election addresses; B.N. Ln. 6. 110]

— *Sénateurs et députés. Silhouettes à la plume* (1876) [B.N. Ln. 6. 111]

Clère, J., *Biographie complète des députés avec toutes les professions de foi* . . . (1877)

Ribeyre, F., *Biographie des sénateurs et des députés* (Angoulême, [1877])

Ribeyre, F., *Biographie des sénateurs et des députés. Nouvelle édition contenant la biographie de tous les nouveaux députés élus les 13 et 28 octobre 1877* (Angoulême [1877])

Clère, J., *Biographie . . . Nouvelle édition augmentée d'un supplement contenant les élections générales du 14 octobre et les élections complémentaires de 1878 et 1879* (1880) [B.N. has only the supplement]

Hourie, P., *Les 557 députés et leurs programmes électoraux 1881–1885* (1882)

[Duquesne, A.,] *Musée national. La Chambre des Députés. Biographies et portraits* (1886) [With 2 maps of 1881 and 1885 elections by departments]

Ribeyre, F., *La Nouvelle Chambre, 1885–1889: Biographie des 584 députés* (1886)

Bertrand, A., *La Chambre de 1889: biographies des 576 députés* . . . (n.d.)

Duguet, E., *Les députés et les cahiers électoraux de 1889* (1890) [Published as the first issue of *Année parlementaire*, of which there is no further trace]

[Duquesne, A.,] *Grand musée national . . . Elections générales de 1889. Biographies et portraits* (1890)

Ribeyre, F., *La Nouvelle Chambre, 1889–1893: Biographie des 576 députés* (1890)

Bertrand, A., *La Chambre de 1893, biographie des 581 députés* . . . (1893)

[Duquesne, A.,] *Grand musée national. La Chambre des Députés, biographies et portraits* . . . (1893)

Georges, H., and Guigonet, J., *La Nouvelle Chambre . . . 581 biographies de députés* (1894)

Grenier, A. S., *Nos députés, 1893–1898* (n.d.) [All four successive editions of this work are found also on large paper.]

Bertrand, A., *La Chambre des Députés (1898–1902) biographies des 581 députés* . . . (1899)

Grenier, A. S., *Nos députés, 1898–1902* (n.d.)

Grenier, A. S. *Nos députés, 1902–1906* (n.d.)

Grenier, A. S. *Nos députés, 1906–1910* (n.d.)

Ripault, E., and Bourreau, R., *La Chambre de 1910. Notices biographiques* . . . (1911)

Normand, G., *Politique et hommes politiques. II. Tout le Parlement: biographies sommaires des sénateurs et députés français au 15 octobre 1924* (1925)

3. — *Biographie des 75 sénateurs inamovibles* (1875) [B.N. Ln. 6. 104—missing]

— *Les sénateurs inamovibles. Notices biographiques . . . par trois journalistes* (1876) [B.N. Ln. 6. 103]

— *Biographie complète des trois cents sénateurs . . . par trois journalistes* (1876) [B.N. Ln. 6. 106]

— *Biographie complète des 300 sénateurs, par un député* (1876) [B.N. Ln. 6. 107]

— *Sénateurs et députés. Silhouettes à la plume.* (1876) [B.N. Ln. 6. 111]

Clère, J., *Biographie complète des sénateurs* (?) [Not in B.N. Known to me only from an advertisement]

Ribeyre, F., *Biographie des sénateurs et des députés* (Angoulême, 1877) [For details, see above, Section 2]

Bertrand, A., *Le Sénat de 1894, biographies des 300 sénateurs* . . . (1894)

[Etard, G.,] *Le Sénat illustré, 1894–1897* (1895)

Grenier, A. S., *Nos sénateurs . . . biographies et portraits (1894–1897)* (1895)

Bertrand, A., *Le Sénat de 1897* . . . (1898)

Grenier, A. S. *Nos sénateurs . . . (1897–1900)* (1899)

Bertrand, A., *Le Sénat de 1900* . . . (1900)

Grenier, A. S. *Nos sénateurs . . . (1900–1903)* (1901)

Grenier, A. S. *Nos sénateurs* . . . *(1903–1906)* (1904)

Grenier, A. S. *Nos sénateurs* . . . *(1906–1909)* (1906)

Normand, G., *Politique et hommes politiques* . . . (1925) [For details, see above, Section 2]

4. [Ereype, P.,] *Assemblée de Versailles. Photographies parlementaires* . . . (1872) [B.N. has first series only, A-Galloni d'Istria]

Dumay, L., *Nos représentants* . . . (Châlons-sur-Marne, 1873) [Covers 127 deputies.] 2 vols.

[Texier, E. A.,] *Portraits de Kel-Kun* (1875)

[Texier, E. A.,] *Nouveaux portraits de Kel-Kun* (1876) [Cover 71 deputies]

— *Biographie des 363* (1877) [B.N. Ln. 6. 114. With a map showing their constituencies]

Vaughan, E., *Le Pilori de l'Intransigeant* (1885) [Covers about 320 deputies]

Bosq, P., *Le Guignol parlementaire* (1902) [Covers 56 deputies]

Damon, L., *Nos parlementaires* (1925) [Covers about 110 parliamentarians]

Damon, L., *Ministres et ministrables* (1926) [Covers about 110 parliamentarians]

— *La foire aux places. Messieurs les députés de la Nièvre* . . . (Bourges, 1872) [B.N. Ln. 6. 95]

— *Biographie des 21 députés de la Seine. Elections du 2 juillet 1871* (1871) [B.N. Ln. 6. 87]

— *Assemblée nationale de Bordeaux. Notices biographiques. Les députés de la Seine* (1871) [B.N. Ln. 6. 91]

— *Biographie des 43 députés de Paris* (1872) [B.N. has only first series (16 deputies); one folio sheet – Ln. 6. 92]

Le Chartier, E., *Les fiches parlementaires* . . . *indiquant les origines de tous les parlementaires du département* . . . (1912) [B.N. has only two issues: Haute-Garonne, Seine-Inférieure]

Chirac, A., *L'Agiotage sous la Troisième Republique* (1888) 2 vols. [Especially Vol. II, pp. 4–9: 50 senators, 100 deputies]

Mennevée, R., *Parlimentaires et financiers*

— — (1922) [Not in B.N.]

— — (1924) [240 parliamentarians]

— — (1925) [202 parliamentarians]

Hamon, A., *Les maîtres de la France* (1936–8) 3 vols. [Especially Vol. II, pp. 303–6: 90 parliamentarians]

— *Album des parlementaires communistes* (1936) [B.N. Ln. 6. 176]

— *La Voix du peuple au parlement. Les 2 sénateurs et les 72 députés communistes.*
(Supplément au No. 12 des *Cahiers du Bolchevisme*) [B.N. Ln. 6. 179–179 C:
all these are identical except in titling on the cover]

5. The "Barodets" are more properly known by the official title of "Recueil
des textes authentiques des programmes et engagements électoraux des
députés proclamés élus . . ." They are to be found in the series of the *Journal
Officiel: Chambre: Documents parlementaires;* they bear a number in the series
of documents of a legislature and are also noted as "Annexe au procès-verbal
de la séance du . . ." They were first issued for the elections of 1881.

1881 – 3ᵉ législature, 1882 No. 808   Annexe . . . 11 novembre 1882
1885 – 4ᵉ législature, 1886 No. 683   Annexe . . . 17 avril 1886
1889 – 5ᵉ législature, 1890 No. 493   Annexe . . . 25 mars 1890
1893 – 6ᵉ législature, 1894 No. 532   Annexe . . . 15 mars 1894
1898 – 7ᵉ législature, 1899 No. 1321 Annexe . . . 23 décembre 1899
1902 – 8ᵉ législature, 1902 No. 1162 Annexe . . . 3 juillet 1902
1906 – 9ᵉ législature, 1907 No. 1090 Annexe . . . 25 juin 1907
1910 – 10ᵉ législature, 1910 No. 385   Annexe . . . 25 octobre 1910
1914 – 11ᵉ législature, 1914 No. 287   Annexe . . . 8 juillet 1914
1919 – 12ᵉ législature, 1920 No. 1431 Annexe . . . 28 juillet 1920
1924 – 13ᵉ législature, 1925 No. 1471 Annexe . . . 26 mars 1925
1928 – 14ᵉ législature, 1930 No. 3814 Annexe . . . 11 juillet 1930
1932 – 15ᵉ législature, 1933 No. 2145 Annexe . . . 27 juin 1933
1936 – 16ᵉ législature: By a resolution of June 8, 1939 this was to be compiled by the staff and no longer by the members of the
Chamber. It was published separately and does not
figure in the *Documents parlementaires.*

6. *Notices et portraits,* otherwise known as the "trombinoscopes", were not put
on sale under the Third Republic, and therefore reached the Bibliothèque
Nationale only haphazardly. More are to be found at the Fondation Nationale des Sciences Politiques (S.P.), but recourse must be had to the libraries of
the Chamber (Ch.) and Senate (S.) and to the archives of the Chamber (Ch.
Arch.).

Notices et portraits appear to have issued for the Chamber from the 9ᵉ législature, for the Senate from 1910.

Chamber: 9ᵉ législature (1908) Ch; Ch. Arch.; S.P
         10ᵉ législature (1911) Ch; Ch. Arch; S.P.
         11ᵉ législature (1916) Ch. Arch; S.P.; B.N.
         also "Edition provisoire" (1914) Ch; S.P.
         12ᵉ législature (1920) Ch. Arch.; S.P.; S.
         13ᵉ législature (1925) Ch.; Ch. Arch.

14ᵉ législature (1929) Ch.; Ch. Arch.
15ᵉ législature (1933) Ch.; Ch. Arch.; S.P.
16ᵉ législature (1936) Ch.; Ch. Arch.; S.P.
16ᵉ législature; Elections partielles (1940) Ch.

Senate: (1910) S.; S.P. B.N.
(1921) S.
(1925) S.
(1930) S.
(1933) S.
(1936) S.; B.N.
(1939) S.; S.P.

INDEX